DOING RELATIONSHIPS
GOD'S WAY

MARJORIE COLE

I Dedicate "Doing Relationships God's Way" to my husband, Jarrol and myself and God who has blessed our lives and used us to be a blessing to each other and fruitful in the service of the Lord for over 50 years.

INTRODUCTION

Life could simply be defined as doing relationships. Relationships are the proving grounds for love. Love is the language of God, the language He is teaching us to speak through relationships. *Doing Relationships God's Way* comes out of abiding in the Vine, the source of our life and strength. As we know we are loved, we can love and forgive one another and live in peace and good will toward our fellow man. All good gifts, including peace and healing, come out of knowing we are loved by God and belong with Him. All of our natural life relationships that come out of knowing we are loved and safe will give us strength and courage to defeat the spirit of fear. Perfect love casts out fear.

Relationships are the source of our greatest blessings and the place of our greatest pain. I realize I have only lightly touched the surface in this matter and surely do not presumed to explore the depths of your pain. It is my prayer that the words on these pages will encourage and inspire you to prevail against our Enemy who has come to steal, kill and destroy every one of us at the very root and core essence of our existence.

Please read and let the Holy Spirit give you wisdom as you fight for those you love, and may the Lord God grant that we all be filled with "the knowledge of His will in all wisdom and spiritual understanding."(Col 1:9)

*A note to the reader: You will find references to the Enemy capitalized to emphasize to the reader that this is not a casual use of the word 'enemy'. Our Enemy is a real, disembodied being that cannot be overlooked or dismissed.

CONTENTS

CHAPTER 1
WHAT IS A RELATIONSHIP?

What is a relationship? The dictionary defines relationships simply as "a connection; a significant connection or similarity between two or more things, or the state of being related to something else". Our connections with each other are formed through words and deeds as expressed in our feelings and behavior toward one another. Relationships can be established through birth, marriage, covenants, and words, and are formed in the context of family, country, church, work, government, business, and civic duty.

Life is full of relationships. Relationships are the essence and expression of life itself. As a matter of fact, life cannot be defined outside of the context of relationships; those connections we have with other people, places, ideas and things. But, even as love cannot exist without an object to love, to live life without being in relationships is not possible.

Our connections with people, our need to love and be loved; to know and be known, and be in meaningful relationships also makes us vulnerable to being hurt, used, controlled and destroyed by those relationships. Relationships can be the source of our greatest joy and the reason for our deepest sorrows. They can bring meaning and definition or bind us in pain and oppression.

Though the dictionary adds nothing to our understanding of relationships in terms of moral obligation or forgiveness or the difficulties that can spring from them, the Bible does. It is THE textbook on relationships. Almost every kind of relationship is described within its pages, including every kind of emotion and physical response, in almost every context imaginable, both good and bad.

Relationships are destroyed when the law of love is broken; when we fail to pay our debt of love to our fellow man, to "owe no man anything but to love one another". The law of love charges us to live peaceably with all men, as much as is possible, as we endeavor to "love our neighbor as we love ourselves". The law of love is the foundation of justice and truth.

Relationships begin with and end up defining family. Families are the basic building blocks of society. One of the Enemy's top priorities and major strategies is the destruction of the family and all it represents. He does this through deception and the destruction of relationships. He works to divide our house and conquer our souls to separate us from one another and the love of God by breaking up our relationships.

And, though the Bible clearly says "we do not wrestle against flesh and blood," (Eph. 6:12); we are constantly looking at each other as the enemy and for a way to prove our point; never recognizing the bigger picture or the depth of the spiritual battle all around us. Even as we live as the redeemed sons and daughters of God in the midst of this present darkness, we become the Enemy's biggest target and greatest opportunity as he tests the hearts of God's people through relationships.

Our greatest efforts to keep the peace and administer justice would be of little effect against his onslaught of lies and aggressive demonic activity, except for the fact that Jesus Christ is with us.

Outside of the authority we have as believers in Jesus Christ, we have no real power over the relentless work of the Thief who has come to steal, kill and destroy our lives, families and relationships.

Countless counseling sessions, church unity movements, self-help books, and teaching and mediation classes have not been able to stop him or resolve the relationship conflicts we experience or bring lasting peace to those caught up in such conflicts. Only the Word of God can show us how to live and give us the courage to love. With that as our truth, we invite you to join us as we look into what the Bible has to say about "Doing Relationships God's Way".

RELATIONSHIPS ARE ROADS

Relationships are not often as simple or straightforward as we would like to believe. There are no short cuts or quick fixes in relationships. Relationships are like tender plants. If they are to thrive and grow they must be cared for specifically and nurtured gently to bring forth pleasing fruit. They must be watered and tended lest they be left to themselves and die.

Relationships are also like roads. They require work and maintenance. They must be kept free of obstructions so those who use them will be able to travel safely upon them. Both roads and relationships connect us with each other and with other elements in our environment that are essential in sustaining life; including the exchange of goods and services vital to the well-being of all of us. And even as relationships form the basic infrastructure that ties the family of man together, those connections can bring safety or death and be in dire need of repair.

If the relationship - the pathway between people - is strewn with broken promises, cruel words, shattered dreams, and hope deferred, walking on them will be painful and destructive. In Hebrews 12:13 the Bible tells us to "make straight paths for our feet, so that what is lame may not be dislocated, but rather be healed". Injustices and rejection break down those spiritual, emotional, and physical roads to tear up the fabric of our souls and isolate us from one another.

Relationships are built with actions and words. Those words and actions become the building blocks that form and shape our self-concept, our worldview and our relationships. As basic and beguine as those words and actions may seem to be, they have the power to give life or destroy it, even to the place of causing some to be lost forever. Because we are all bound together and defined by our relationships their power to either tear us down or build us up is a principle factor in defining life itself.

Words can bath our life in hope or drown it in sorrow. Words cut down grown men or shape the precious, irreplaceable souls of children, first knit together in the matrix of a mother's womb by the gentle hand of God. What deadly and unimaginable power the Creator has put into the hands of those who will first care for those children. To think that their identity and their sense of well-being, including the determination of their eternal destiny, will be based on the data they gather from those around them.

We are all in danger of being loved conditionally and judged by the expectations and perceptions of those around us. We are judged, not within the context of our need for love and honor and acceptance, but from within the context of a harsh and unloving worldview that springs from distrust and breeds insecurity. In that worldview, there are two sets of rules, one for those given over to the influences of evil and the other for those given over to the pursuit of God. This dual system creates untold opportunities for injustice and offense to destroy and dissolve relationships.

HEALTHY, HAPPY, HOLY RELATIONSHIPS

For a relationship to be happy it must be healthy. For a relationship to be healthy, it must be holy, founded and based in the truth of God's Holy Word. Who I am is not based upon what I think I am or I am not, or on what others say about me. It is based on what God says about me.

Only the Creator Himself can assign worth and value to me. He determines my worth by the price He was willing to pay to buy me back from the grip of the 'terrible one." (Is. 49: 25) That price was fully paid by the Blood of God who gave His life for my life - the death of God for the life of me.

God is the One Who authorized my existence in the first place. He is the One Who has the final word defining me and what I am worth. My value cannot come from the opinions of others who, like myself, are finite and fitted into the same frame of reference and pressed by the same needs as I. The revelation of that truth must come from a source that is both outside of us and greater than us.

Jesus likens this generation to "children sitting in the marketplace and calling to one another, saying; 'We played the flute for you, and you did not dance; we mourned to you, and you did not weep.' (Lu. 7:31-32) Though the opinions and expectations of others put us under much peer pressure to perform according to other people's standards, they do not form the essence of our true character or nature.

The true revelation of who we are comes from God. When Jesus asked His disciples "Who do men say that I am?" Peter answered saying, "You are the Christ, the Son of the living God." (Mt. 16:16) Jesus answered and said to him, "Blessed are you, Simon Bar-Jonah, for flesh and blood has not revealed this to you, but My Father who is in heaven." (Mt. 16:17) Peter had received the revelation from heaven in his spirit that bore witness to his mind and heart.

Notice that as Peter gained a deeper revelation of Who Christ was, he gained a deeper understanding of who he was, as well. 'Simon, Bar-Jonah', "I say to you that you are Peter," (Mt. 16:18). He gained a deeper revelation of who he was from knowing Who God is.

To know who I am, I must know Him. To know Him, I must spend time with Him in His Word. The revelation and Word of Jesus is the true and final truth of who I am, because, then, even if my heart condemns me, as the scripture says, "God is greater than my heart and knows all things." (I Jn. 3:20) God knows my heart and His judgment supersedes even my own heart's fears, feelings and judgments.

THE THREE CORE ISSUES OF LIFE IN RELATIONSHIPS

The three basic questions we must all answer that form the core of our life's work in relationships can be reduced to three primary issues. The three basic tasks in life are to resolve the issues of safety, righteousness, and responsibility. Whether we acknowledge it or not, those issues become the driving force and motivation behind our words and actions in our connections and exchanges with others.

By very virtue of being alive on the earth, each of us must address the need for personal safety, the establishment of our individual righteousness, and answer the question of whose responsibility is it. Because we will solve these problems using information we have learned from our parents, peers and early caregivers, our beliefs will come from them.

This means nothing changes much from one generation to the next unless there is a divine intervention of truth that alters and adjusts the information that has been learned and handed down, to match the truth of what God says. If the information we received is flawed or false, our abilities to resolve the challenges of life will be unsatisfactory and unsatisfying.

To complicate the matter, each of these issues is presented to us in the context of fear or faith. Both faith and fear make a compelling argument in an effort to persuade us to embrace their version of the story life tells us. The power of faith and the power of fear both demand to be fulfilled and insist they be heard. Both would persuade us they bring the truth and offer us the best solution to the problem.

Using the information presented to us by our souls through the use of our minds and emotions does not allow us to make a confident or good choice. Using a sloppy combination of reasoning and reality obscures the truth about what God wants us to know. Yielding to doubt and fear only creates inconsistency in our words and actions that make it difficult to untangle the messages or understand the motives we send and receive in our relationships.

SAFETY

The issue of safety springs out of our desire to live and succeed. Survival and the desire to live are a motivating force found in the soul of every living, breathing thing, God created. Human beings are no exception. Because we are born fragile and defenseless and forced to depend on others for the provision of our early needs, infancy and childhood can be an extremely dangerous and difficult time.

The urgency of securing food, warmth and love create pressure in the environmental boxes that shape and control our lives as we struggle to stay alive. Our young self is like soft clay, still impressionable and extremely vulnerable to the pressure at work within the box. We feel anxious and abandoned. We feel alone and begin to strive, to manage or make-do.

Children pick up the mind-sets and behaviors of their early care-givers and suspect nothing amiss. And though those circumstances might have been inadequate and destructive, they set in motion the dynamics that define the child's belief systems and mold him or her into who they will become; things they will spend the rest of their lives trying to forget and undo.

Eventually, many of us give up and settle into an agreement with the Enemy in any one of a number of ways he uses to obligate us to enter into a contract with fear. We begin to experience our lives in the context of other people's pain and dysfunction. We take on their hurt and anger and try to fix them so our lives can be safe and fulfilled.

We swallow and stuff the injustices they put upon us and learn to pretend or take on the desired 'persona' required to stay alive, be loved and stay out of trouble. Eventually, we deny ourselves and trade our identity for survival. As unfair and unfortunate as that is, our lives are more determined by the dispositions of those around us than by any specific decisions we first make about a matter.

RIGHTEOUSNESS

Our second task is to resolve the question of righteousness, which includes the establishment of our right to be here and what we are worth. Included in the right to be here is the right to be loved and be seen as righteous. The problem of our righteousness began when Satan took over the dominion of the earth through the sin of Adam and Eve. He changed our definition from 'beings' to 'doings'. We were created by the Supreme Being as human beings made in the image of the One Who created us.

When the Devil stole the Kingdom from Adam and Eve, he redefined them as slaves, as 'human doings'. That definition became the underlying principal that controls everything, including the thoughts we have about ourselves. Living in this world where all of 'who we are', including our righteousness, is determined by what we do and how well we are doing it sets us up perfectly for the Enemy's plan to steal our souls .

All the Enemy has to do to get us to sin is to get us to believe his lie and use his solution to solve our problems. The moment we enter into the agreement to use the Devil's solutions to our 'problems' we are under his control. The Enemy of our soul uses our innate divine nature that hates sin and injustice, to get us to try harder to be good. We are caught between feeling guilty for sinning and feeling justified in trying to do better, only to be overcome by failure and condemnation.

Using our desire to establish our own righteousness (goodness), the Enemy tangles us up with trying to 'be good' and getting other people to acknowledge that goodness. Trying to reestablishing our righteousness reflects our struggle over the loss of our position in God's divine order and life's effort to re-establish our divine nature as being made in the image of God; the revelation of which was severely compromised in 'the Fall.'

We wrestle with questions of goodness and morality. How do I establish my righteousness in the midst of a fallen world where sin and depravation rule in the hearts and affairs of men? How do I be good in a world filled with evil? What can I do to restore my relationship with my heavenly Father when I may not even know that I have a Father in Heaven? How do the judgments I make about myself in comparing myself with others and their treatment of me establish my righteousness? How does judging others affect my view of them and how I treat them?

RESPONSIBILITY

The treatment of others raises the third issue, which opens up the question of responsibility. Whose job is it? Whose fault is it?

Who's to blame? To fix something we must first identify the problem. Many of us spend years troubleshooting our lives or the lives of others to find something or someone to blame for what has happened to us. Blaming is as old as humanity. Adam blamed Eve and Eve blamed the snake. It offers convincing evidence that the deadly effect the curse has had upon human relationships is real and present.

The attempt to place blame has scattered the contents of Pandora's box all over the landscape of human relationships. To this very day, we grapple with ethics and morality. Our court systems are filled with lawsuits and angry petitioners who are seeking justice and the restoration of their human dignity. But, even if we can find someone to blame, which sometimes includes ourselves, the real question is not a question of who is responsible. Pointing the finger does not put the issue of responsibility to rest or resolve the issues of justice as long as the real Enemy still lies hidden beneath the pile of demonic accusations he is eager to press against us.

Questions of civic duty and social obligation such as, whose job is it to take care of the world or make it safe for others, remain unanswered. We are driven to resolve the issues of innocence and personal justifications by asking questions like; Whose fault is it? Who should pay for it? Who can I sue? When is it my turn? All of these questions only turn into irresolvable conflicts and unfinished arguments. Where does my responsibility end and another's begin? Who will help me? Why isn't it fair? These are all questions that divide and drive our relationships to deeper places of pain and pressure.

We have been trained to ask the wrong questions in our pursuit of peace and justice. God does not admonish us to judge one another and thereby absolve ourselves from wrong doing. Instead, He tells us to confess our sins and repent. We are to cancel out our agreements with the lies. Those agreements have only produced the sin we now seek to rid ourselves of. Our allegiance to the Liar who wants to put the blame for the sin onto us or get us to blame each other must be broken.

When we agree with guilt instead of confessing our sin to God, the Enemy uses guilt and feeling guilty to get us to believe that, because we sinned, we are responsible to deal with that sin. That is true, but the Enemy uses that obligation to divert us from the real issue Those around us have also been trained to reinforce the concept of us taking the responsibility for our behavior, again reinforcing the cardinal rule of the Snake Pit, i.e., 'you are what you do'.

TAKING RESPONSIBILITY

As Satan gets us to 'own' and take the responsibility for 'our' sin, which so many of us are told is the 'right thing' to do, we become defeated. If we think we can out-last or out-wit the devil with 'will power' and 'self-control' and more discipline, we are tricked into taking on a battle that we cannot win; a battle that has already been fought and won for us by the Lord, Jesus Christ.

The average Christian believes that repentance and taking responsibility are essentially the same things, but they are not. The Bible does not teach us, nor did Jesus ever say, 'You need to take responsibility for your sin.' He did say, "The kingdom of God is at hand. Repent and believe in the gospel". (Mk. 1:15) Taking responsibility means being obedient to do what the Lord says to do.

We are told to repent, but repentance comes after we receive a revelation of our sin, either through the Word, or by the conviction of the Holy Spirit, or both. Repentance is acknowledging that we have sinned. We sinned because we believed lies. In repentance we acknowledge our need for forgiveness, that we cannot set ourselves free or 'be good enough to get to heaven' apart from Jesus Christ. His death and resurrection set us free and establish us in His righteousness.

Taking responsibility for our sin would ultimately requires that we die for our own sin. If Satan can convince me, I am the sin I hate, then, to get rid of the sin, I must get rid of myself. If it is true that I am a liar, a thief, or a pervert then to get rid of lying, stealing and perversion, Satan's proposal is for me to get rid of myself! This is the Enemy's solution to the sin problem. But how does my agreement with the Enemy to get rid of myself, solve the problem of sin in my life? And ultimately, how does my destroying myself profit the Kingdom of God?

Paul recognizes the trap Satan has set for him and cries out, "O wretched man that I am! WHO will deliver me from this body of death?" (Rom. 7:24) He knew he was no match for the Enemy or his accusation. He realized that no matter how much responsibility he took, nothing is ever going to be enough to satisfy the Accuser.

The same God that commands us to repent, did not take this 'golden opportunity' to set the record straight and admonish us to 'take responsibility' for thing that was dwelling in us that was causing us to do those things we 'willed not' to do, (sin). We are instructed through the same words and example Paul used when he himself cried out for 'deliverance'.

We have all been taught to 'take responsibility for our actions'. But, as reasonable as 'taking responsibility' sounds, the word 'responsibility' is NOT found in the Bible. The idea of 'taking responsibility' for our sin is a man-made tenant of faith not endorsed in the Word of God. When Paul, the writer to the Romans, discovers the entrapment of doing the things he doesn't want to do, (Rom. 7:20) he did not exhort himself or us to take responsibility or try harder to overcome sin through more self-control. He flat out says, 'the thing he was doing that he did not want to do, was NOT him!' He said it was the 'sin' that dwelt IN him.

We conclude that Paul did not find 'taking personal responsibility' to be a very helpful thing in his battle against the evil that dwelt within him. He realized that he was still a "wretched man" (Rom. 7:23-24) even after he recognized he was not creating the war that was going on inside of him. It was not him doing it! The division and confusion in Paul's mind was cleared up by turning the battle over to his Defender and realizing that "by the grace of God, I am what I am". (I Cor. 12:15) His sin had been forgiven. He no longer tried to come up with a remedy for his own soul by asking WHAT he must do?

He realized that God's solution to sin was deliverance and that he could in no way, take care of this thing himself. This revelation forced him to rest in the finished work of Christ on the Cross. He came to the glorious conclusion he shared with us, that no matter what we feel like or no matter what we think, "there is therefore now, no condemnation to those who are in Christ Jesus who do not walk according to the flesh, but according to the Spirit." (Rom. 8:1)

The issue of condemnation had been addressed in the death and resurrection of the One Who paid the price. We, like the Apostle Paul, need a deliverer. Jesus Christ is our deliverer; the One Who rescues and sets us free from the one who persecutes our soul and has tried to separate us from the love of God our Savior through sin.

Understanding who we are in Christ and our new position in Him shifts our relationship with sin from one of bondage to one of liberty. The ruling of the grace of God overturns the case sin had built against us in the Court of Heaven and the strongholds it had created in our soul. Christ gives us firm footing through His forgiveness from which to stand and from which to "fight the good fight of faith." (II Tim. 4:7)

From the moment of salvation, we are given the choice to follow Christ and allow Him to work in us both to 'will and do of His good pleasure'. We rest in Him and through Christ; we have been reinstated to the position of son and servant, a soldier of the Cross, and a defender of the faith. We are given the choice we never had before, the option to abide instead of hide - to live in freedom instead of enslavement.

* * *

CHAPTER 2
MY RELATIONSHIP WITH GOD

Who is God? Is He sovereign? Is He cruel? Is He kind? Does He know everything before it happens? Does He care about me? How can He be all knowing and all good and all-powerful and still let all these awful things happen even to innocent people?

If our concept of God is wrong, our relationship with Him cannot be right. If we see Him as angry and unforgiving, we will be vulnerable to believing we are on our own, or that we must please Him to get Him to like us. We will believe Satan's description of God and the lies he has told us, instead of listening and looking into 'Who God is' for ourselves.

No other Being in the universe has been blamed more often for the problems on earth and taken the hits for its failures than God. Satan has spared no expense in making God the justification for religious cruelty, His name a common curse word, and the reason for everything that is wrong in this world. (Never mind the fact that God has given us a free will and that the messes we have made are the consequences of decisions we have made ourselves).

Some would defend God as patient and kind, which He obviously is, since He sends the rain on the just and on the unjust, and is long-suffering, "not willing that any should perish". Others criticize God as unresponsive and distant. A remote and disinterested God is not the kind of God we need, even though many have foolishly dismissed having a relationship with God as either unnecessary or too controlling.

Others make excuses for God, or manipulate their relationship with Him in order to control Him. Trying to explain Who He is and why He does the things He does outside of the context of the Holy Scriptures is conjecture and assumption. Building our descriptions of God and His character according to our own perceptions is no different than our creating any one of the many false gods and setting them up as the idols we worship. Worshipping anything we have declared to be God that is not, is only a figment of our fear or our vain imagination, and is idolatry.

Our inability to understand who God is, however, has left the foundation of our relationship with our Father unstable and easily shaken. This has caused huge problems for both God and us, as He does not often come down and defend Himself. And because His ways are higher than our ways and His thought than our thoughts, we are quickly confused and upset about the things He does or does not do, and the way He carried out His acts as God.

For too many, God, the Creator of Heaven and Earth, who desires to be in relationship with us as our Father is seen as stern and severe or as fickle and uncaring. A great cloud of confusion and theological discussion hangs over Him that causes the timid and unseasoned to believe what they are told about God, if they believe anything about Him at all. Few know what God says about Himself. To make matters worse, scriptures is a two edged sword which means, scripture can be used to argued against scripture. This ends up frustrating the learner and discouraging the disciple even more.

IN DEFENSE OF JUSTICE

God's character is displayed in His love and in His justice. Many scriptures talk about the judgment of the wicked and the severity of God. No isolated scripture bearing witness to His love or His justice, however, can be correctly interpreted if it is interpreted to contradict other scriptures about God, or is chosen to the exclusion of the other. God is both good and loving and just and severe. Like any honorable parent who both can be seen holding and comforting his child, as well as, disciplining him, God's heart is always 'for us', no matter what things may look like at times during the relationship.

We are admonished to "rightly divide the word of truth." (II Tim. 3:15-16) As a matter of fact, in this same place where we are admonished to rightly divide the word of truth we are also warned not to "strive about words to no profit, to the ruin of the hearers." Truth is like a coin. It must have both 'heads' and 'tails' to be genuine and complete.

Many theologies and the denominations have come out of striving about 'words to the hurt and harm of the hearers'. For this reason, God is pleased to send the Holy Spirit Who will lead us into all truth and triumph. He has been sent to guide us into the revelation of Jesus Christ and through the scriptures, to give us a deeper understanding of who He is.

Much of the activity that centers around the scriptures, however, is not God-guided, or Holy Ghost revelation, but rather, an endless discussion to further entangle the listeners, spear-headed by demons, religious spirits and doctrines of demons. (I Tim. 4:1-3) It is propaganda meant to divide and dishearten the church of Jesus Christ corporately, and its members individually.

DEFINING GOD

Down through the ages and in each dispensation, great pains have been taken to define God and His character. The majority of these attempts have not based their reasoning and conclusions upon scripture, but upon tradition, opinion and superstition. They are designed for politics gain and control of the masses. Even the most sincere efforts and beginnings have morphed into grotesque religious monstrosities that cause the people to labor under countless unnecessary "burdens too grievous to be born". (Mt. 23:1-4)

The tragic irony of these efforts has been to promote a distorted concept of God generated by an unholy worldview that has ended up separating us from Him and one another. The Enemy has controlled all the narratives, including our thoughts towards God and the necessity of His relevance in our lives. The bitter disputes have rendered our pursuit of God as both treacherous and in some cases deadly, leaving both martyrs and heretics in its wake.

It is just as Jesus Christ told us. We have been set us up in such opposition to ourselves and each other (II Tim. 2:24-26 JKV) that we fail miserably to keep God's most basic commandment to love one another. Instead we have killed each other, burned one another at the stake, torn apart families, started civil wars, or lit others on fire to be used as human torches, thinking all the while we are doing God a service. How twisted!

How brutal and blind Satan has made us, to think that doing such things pleases God and proves our loyalty to Him. What kind of a God would our Father be, if these were the kind of things He required of us? How is He any different than the pagan idols to whom human sacrifices were offered? Even to this very day we do not see the great suffering we have brought upon one another because of the religion beliefs that blind us to the truth.

Even as we have refused the love of the truth, blinded by the lies we hold to be true, we take no responsibly or express remorse for enforcing such atrocities and pain upon our fellow human beings. "And for this reason, God will send them strong delusion, that they should believe the lie, that they all may be condemned who did not believe the truth but had pleasure in unrighteousness." (II Thess. 2:11-12)

If we have a wrong concept of God, we are serving a wrong god. Our service will not be out of love and devotion, but out of fear and patronizing. Though the Bible says the "fear of the Lord is the beginning of wisdom," (Pr. 9:10) God is not an invisible tyrant who wants to conceal Himself, who delights in sneaking up on us with a huge baseball bat of misfortune to teach us a lesson on how to trust Him.

If we have the wrong concept of God and serve Him out of fear, we will have a cold hearted and emotionless God that only cares about the rules and not the relationship. On the other hand, if we have a soft grace-gushing God Who is too afraid to correct us we will have a wimpy, tongue-tangled Gospel that sets us apart as nothing different than the world we seek to correct.

If our concept of God is not the truth as He reveals Himself through the scripture and the Holy Spirit, we will have no authority or confidence in Him or His promises. Instead of confidence in God and His faithfulness, we will find ourselves giving up on God and being reabsorbed into the world. Once liberated and enlightened, we will find ourselves now living in a wrong Gospel and a false peace. We will carry a form of godliness that even those who deny God can see through. They will hold us in contempt and call us weak. They will label us as hypocrites as they have yet to see, in most of us who call ourselves Christians, fearless love lived out in the true heart of Christ.

The One True God, as He has revealed Himself through the Bible and His prophets, as revealed through Jesus Christ, and as given to us through the Holy Spirit, lives! He is not lost or confused about Who He is or what His job is. We are the ones who are lost and in need of clarification. The best place to find the answers and get our concept of God straightened out requires that we go back to the beginning and take a closer look at what He told us.

THE ABC'S OF CREATION

In the beginning, as recorded in Genesis, we are introduced to three key sets of players represented as God, (the Trinity); Satan, (including his company of fallen angels); and Adam and Eve, the first set of humans, made in the image of God.

We know the story, at least enough to piece together the general highlights of what happened. Adam and Eve, innocent and only aware of goodness and God, suspected nothing contrary to His good will and generous Spirit toward them. The garden was perfect, wonderful, warm, and safe. They knew nothing of evil, either from within themselves, or from without. To say that they were innocent and naïve, totally sheltered and unaware of evil is an understatement. They had NO clue. All they had was God's stern warning NOT to eat or touch the tree or the fruit of the tree of the Knowledge of Good and Evil.

As the Bible describes it, there had been a war in Heaven and Lucifer, the chief worship leader of heaven had been cast out. He became the chief of a third of the angels who followed him in that revolution. Lucifer, now called Satan, along with these fallen angels, were looking for a place to call their own. Seeing the vulnerability of God's newly created, 'pride and joy', inspired the envy of this Evil One. He seized his opportunity to capture their kingdom and subdue them by taking on the form of one of the garden creatures, a talking snake.

The Serpent began to dialogue with Eve. We are not told anything that would strike us as alarming or lead us to suspect that Eve had been harboring a desire in her heart for greatness or personal gain as the serpent Satan had. She seemed to have no idea that her pursuit of God, as demonstrated in her desire to 'know more', would lead her to consume the fruit on the forbidden tree, or end up in death and eternal disaster for so many of her children.

A GOOD HEART

Her heart was not created in the image of evil nor could it comprehend the danger of the evil that stood facing her. "Let us make man in our image," (Gen. 1:26-27) God said. Nothing else, of all His creation had been given such specific attention. He created cattle, and creeping things, and fish and fowl, and the "stars also", but nothing is said of any of their essence or image being made in His likeness, or even of His intention in creating them.

The creatures and their habitats were created by Him, for His enjoyment. They were made to stock and populate the place He had prepared for His children. God knew Lucifer would be an unending threat to the innocence of His children who lived sheltered away in the safety of the Garden of Eden. He knew it was only a matter of time before the Evil One would set his sights on them, to snatch them up and try to devour them. And indeed, what God knew would happen, did happen!

Adam and Eve had no motive for evil or to bring hurt to anyone. They were not created innately evil nor did they want evil for any one else. They were created by God and carried His likeness; a divine nature that loved justice, truth and mercy.

But, in spite of the peace and beauty of their surroundings and God's provision in supplying all their needs in abundance, they were tempted. In spite of His command not to eat the fruit of the Tree of the Knowledge of Good and Evil, the Serpent found a way to tempt them to disobey God.

Was it their desire to be wise or did they see the fruit as harmless? Was it Eve's desire to be more 'like God' that finally caused her to touch and then taste the fruit? When Adam and Eve ate the fruit of the tree of the Knowledge of Good and Evil they realized they were naked and were ashamed. Before they could even grasp what had happened, Satan twisted God's divine warning, "the soul that sins shall die" (Ezk. 18:4) into his own demonic judgment to demand they pay the consequences of that warning. Death set in and evil took ahold of their lives!

They had been deceived. They had disobeyed and been enticed into listening to the one who had tempted them to sin against God's command to not eat the forbidden fruit. Original sin ruptured the relationship they had had with God. Separation and sin entered into the world. They felt the sting of its death, even as the shame of it drove them to cover themselves with fig leaves and hide from God.

For the first time in their lives, they felt alone and afraid of God. Sin tore apart their innocence and reduced their desperate desire to regain that goodness to a tiny glimmer of hope and a life-sentence of regret and striving to be good. Guilt and shame hammered a wedge between them and God that alienated them and altered their own sense of goodness. They were driven out of their home and began wandering in a foreign and hostile place, homeless and lost.

THE SNAKE PIT

They had fallen into the Snake Pit where the Serpent ruled. Their innocence and beauty - the glory of their divine nature - which was their original nature, was now covered over in the slime of the Pit. Sin and Satan had succeeded in reducing them to a shadow of their former selves. Their remembrance of their divine nature began to grow dim. Their understanding and fellowship with God began to fade.

They were being physically and psychologically redefined and programmed by the "body of death" to believe they were 'doings' and not 'beings'. Their divine nature was completely re assigned and overtaken by the man-made idea of a 'sinful human nature'.

The sons and daughters of God were now identified with a 'sinful human nature' that obscured their divine nature and set them up as perfect candidates for the lies Satan would use to catch them in the nets of religion. They began to live in opposition to each other, themselves and God. They worked and fought and were taught to believe lies that caused them to reject the love of God and alienate them from His truth.

That human nature gave them a different view of life and a different way of approaching everything. Fueled by reason and bound by reality, they became the victims of religion. They were cursed into having to earn their bread by the sweat of their brow. No longer could they just pick of life's sweet goodness, eat and be satisfied. Labor and futility and exhaustion became their taskmasters. They were thrust into a new paradigm, one of trying to recover their righteousness and innocence by 'being good'.

Satan sent Hell's counselors, Reasoning, Reality, Responsibility and Religion to instruct them, to tempt them, to use their 'hunger for home', to bait them and catch them on the hooks of Hell . He set up the torture racks of trying to resolve the irresolvable issues of life to pull them apart. Every move them made to try and free themselves from the grip of Satan only pulled them farther into the jaws of the "terrible one" and deeper into the quick sand of the Snake Pit as they tried to get back their original sinless nature.

DARK SHADOWS OF RELIGION

Adam and Eve knew something terrible had happened. A dark shadow fell across their lives and that of their children. Religion subjected them to an endless list of do-good behaviors that only fueled Satan's insatiable contempt for them and wore them out. And even though guilt began to pull them away from goodness and the Enemy tormented them with their sin, the Bible gives no indication that their divine nature was removed or exchanged for a sinful one or that they had become depraved.

They had sinned. But nowhere did God indicate that He had changed His mind or agree with the Enemy's new definition of His children as depraved. God had warned Cain that sin was "crouching at the door" (Gen. 4:7 ESV) of his life as it would now be with all of His children. God knew where His children had come from and He wanted them back. They had been carried away by a mudslide of transgression, into a pit of ruin.

Their (our) plight became the inspiration for the greatest rescue operation ever undertaken since the beginning of time. God saw no need to throw away the child that had been brought down and defiled by the mud (sin) of the Snake Pit. They were, after all, redeemable, washable and precious. God had determined to wash them clean and give a new robe of righteousness - without spot or wrinkle - to 'whosoever' wanted one.

God went after them. He considered them worth the effort. He was committed to them. His love would not let them go. He would bring them back because they were His children, not because they deserved it. Jesus was part of the rescue plan. He fully expressed the heart of the Father in coming to this earth. He came to "seek and save that which was lost," (not that which was rotten and worthless). Would He ever have sought to save something that was bad, if getting rid of it would have been better than saving it?

If something we loved dearly were lost, would we not seek diligently to find it to get back that which was precious to us? We never stopped being precious to God, not for a moment, not even when we did not know or care about His love for us. Sin has not changed our value or the truth of our being or made us into a worthless piece of rubbish unworthy of redemption and a waste of God's time. God's plan of redemption was in fact, an incredible rescue operation He undertook to overcome the power of sin and conquer death. He had to bring restoration and redemption to the lost Kingdom of earth and those who lived there.

So, why didn't He just bring His precious offspring to heaven right away and spare everyone the human tragedy Hell was preparing? Because He had a plan – a plan to install His Son as the King of Kings and the Lord of Lords over all creation. To do that, His Son would have to be proven worthy in His willingness to lay down His life in exchange for ours. Only the substitution of His life for ours would satisfy the demands of the devil and the death he demanded. Only the Death of the spotless, sinless, Lamb of God could reinstate God's children to a place of fellowship with the Father

THE TIDE OF EVIL

Through out history we have seen the tide of evil ebb and flow as the flood of wickedness has covered the earth with an ocean of iniquity and injustice. We have seen sin's effects upon all creation and must agree that even the most innocent is not exempt from suffering under the reign of the god of this world. His contempt for God has altered the course of nations and swallowed up whole civilizations.

God's justice has required His continual intervention in the affairs of men, and though God's way of addressing the "overflow of wickedness" is specific to each generation, it was, and is, all summed up in the Cross. God's intervention in human affairs was made when the cup of His wrath was full. The Bible is full of stories of sin and the vile acts of wickedness that brought plagues and captivity and judgment from the hand of God.

Many only saw God as One filled with anger and indignation, bloody wars and bloody sacrifices made to placate a bloody God. Their fear of Him was more than their love for Him. Sin seemed to have won the battle of stealing the hearts of men and turning them away from the heart of God.

Then the silence came. It was as if the relationship between God and man had ended. There was no clear word from God. It was as if He had nothing more to say to us. All we could do was what we had always done, wait - wait and wonder - and once in a while, remember, until ..., "the fullness of time" (Gal.4:4) finally came, and brought the promise – Jesus, the Lamb of God sent to die, to take away the sins of the world.

Jesus came, taking on the form of a man. He came to earth, full of compassion and truth. This Son of Man, who was also the Son of God was the only One qualified to mediate the great and dreadful divide between God and Man and heal the mortal wound between them. He did not despise His us, though we did not recognize Him or give Him honor. He did not curse those who crucified Him. He cured them and cried for them, and forgave them on the grounds of ignorance.

He did not hold them guiltless for the willful, intentional, premeditated acts of evil they committed against Him, though He took upon Himself the full responsibility for their redemption. He told them of the Father's love and though He knew what was in man, He did not hate him. (Jn. 2:24-25) He saw us for who we really were, the lost sons and daughters of the Most High who He had come to redeem and restore back to our Father, the One Who made us.

THE GOD OF MY FATHERS

Looking briefly at my own childhood, I remember kneeling in the big ornate church where I attended Mass and received holy communion five or six days every week for most of my young life. I was a devout child who modeled myself after the saints, many of whom I knew to have been martyrs, and tried to be as good as they were. I was fully convinced that being good would get me into heaven.

At the end of each day, I would judge myself to see if my good deeds for the day had out-weighed my bad ones. Fortunately, for me, the totals were re-tallied every day, and I was pretty sure I would get through the big gate, with a gentle nod from St. Peter when I died. The golden balance of justice and Peter at the Gate were very vivid childhood images.

Many afternoons, I would kneel in the quiet, empty sanctuary, with the soft smells of the morning incense still hanging in the air, waiting for my ride home from school. It was a parochial school, much like many others, where the fearful black suited nuns represented the holy things of God, even when they did very mean and unholy things. I would sit intently and peer silently into the well-cut faces of the beautiful stone statues of Jesus and Mary and Joseph. But in every sanctuary I had ever visited, there was never a statue of God. I could only wonder what He must look like or be like. The only glimpse I had ever seen of Him appeared as a shaft of bright light in one of the colored pictures on the flip chart of Adam and Eve were being driven out of the Garden of Paradise.

Once I saw a drawing of Him in a catechism. He looked kind enough, but very old, probably ancient because He had been around for such a long time already. His skin was white and He had a very long wispy white beard with a lot of light shining behind His head. That was all I knew of God. He may have looked Fatherly, enough, though I was fully convinced that He was not that interested in listening to children or answering their prayers.

That was Mary's job or one of the saints, and so, as would be expected, most of my attention was focused upon the Queen Mother. She always looked nice and was said to like children. I was taught she was the one who took the place of an intercessor, the one who would go to Jesus to get Him to do stuff. As for Jesus, I was not quite sure who He was or what He did. He was mostly the baby I stared at in the manger every Christmas trying to figure out how He got from the crib to the cross.

GAPS IN THE PICTURE

Needless to say, there were a lot of gaps in my theological under-standing of God, though my intentions were sincere enough. Looking back I can see I was immersed in a system of religion that held very tightly to the things it taught and did not permit anyone to tamper with its sanctioned interpretation of God. All of this left me at a bit of a loss as to how to have a 'personal relationship' with Him.

He was a God to be feared and left alone. He had had His Own Son sacrificed which made Him scary and treacherous enough to make any relationship with Him stressful. If all that He required was never enough, there would be no end point or little rest because all that was done had to be done again the next day. Little did I know how closely this futility matched that of the Levitical priesthood and sacrifices of the Old Testament. Their daily offer-ings of lambs and keeping of laws was really a lot like the closed system I found myself born and locked into.

If our concept of God is one of indifference or impulsivity and unpredictable and punitive wrath, with no apparent way to appease Him, we resort to the primitive ways that the heathen used in appeasing their gods. They offered sacrifices of food and flesh to make their lifeless idols happy never suspecting these sticks and stones and sculpted figures were animated by demons. They worshipped and served these gods out of fear not love.

The Devil introduced these demon gods to our ancestors and used intimidation to get them to give their power over to these evil spirits and disembodied beings. These demonic entities used fear to motivate and control the people demanding sacrifices and offerings in exchange for protection. The people would have to appease the demons with offerings of food and other things that were demanded of them, to garner favor, fertility and protection from the power of these jealous, hateful, and insecure gods. Halloween's 'Trick or Treat', have their roots in these ancient forms of Druidism that used threats and bribery to enslave people in the Kingdom of Darkness.

If God's Enemy can get us to believe God is mean and mad, it makes perfect sense for the Evil One to create and preach a gospel based on fear. He seeks to scare people into being good if they want to get to heaven and by threatening them with Hell if they are bad. The law becomes not only the measuring rod of behavior and the criteria for escaping the flames of Hell, it also makes behavior and good works the primary means for getting the Heaven.

The required sacrifices needed to be made are shifted off the one made by the Lamb of God onto the ones Satan demands of us. In one seemingly subtle and insignificant move, Satan has shifted the core message of the Gospel from the 'Son' dying in my place, to me getting rid of my 'sin' myself. To one consumed with getting rid of his/her own sin, love is not seen as a legitimate way of salvation and grace will be scoffed at. The One true God is mocked and His gift is trampled into the ground by a stampede of fearful worshippers who refuse to believe He loves them and has willingly laid down His life to redeem them.

If we would work to instill fear and dread into our earthly relationships, how many of our loved ones would love us more? How did that work for you as a child, those of you who grew up in an abusive home; where your parent fought and inflicted the overflow of their rage and bitterness onto you? You may have tried harder to be good to stay out of trouble and anticipated their next move to prepare yourself for the worst, but it did not make you feel safe or draw you closer to them.

As a matter of fact, the more we are told one thing and experience the opposite, the more confused and angry we will become. And though I was fortunate to have good parents, just and kind, for many, there is no clear expectation or direction. They are at the mercy of whatever spiritual force controlled their circumstances and their parents. They live, even as Christians, seeking to come up with a plan that would please an angry God and another path that would get them to Heaven.

EARTHLY FATHERS

The relationship we have with our earthly father is a primary relationship. As a primary relationship, it forms the basis for all subsequent relationships, including those we will have with God and other authority figures. Our linage is determined from our earthly father. Our first sets of circumstances and our financial status which shape a great part of who we think we are and how we define ourselves comes from our first parents. Our fathers hold a place of power for both good and evil in our lives. As newborns, we have no say as to who that man will be and though we may look a lot like him, we may not like him at all.

As infants and children, and young adults, we are soft and impressionable, like wet clay. Things can be written on us that will mark and shape us for the rest of our lives. Those critical first impressions, for better or worse, are made by our parents. The power of their words and actions impart the initial information we will use in forming the life-world view we will carry the rest of our life. They set the foundation and provide the infra-structure for our belief systems and mindsets yet to be formed.

Because we do not initially know God or even our being born and brought into existence as anything more than an irrelevant, distant, non-event, our world becomes the faces of those who greet us. It becomes colored and animated through the words, expressions and actions of the people around us. If those greetings are joyous we rejoice. If those greetings and interactions are hostile, we retreat. Many of us are still grieving over the first issues that we encountered as children, conditions that have never been settled, and parents that have never been pleased, all of which continue to be a source of great pain in our adult lives.

These issues include questions of:

- Worth and value, lovability and desirability. (Am I loved and wanted?)
- Failure to meet parent's approval, failure to fix parents.
- Confusion as to why I am not loved, valued, wanted.
- I'm different, I am bad, I am not good enough.
- Conditional love, feeling unloved, I don't deserve.
- Purposelessness – I'm in the way, I'm a bother, I don't matter, I'm no good.
- Responsible for my parent's happiness
- It's my fault, I'm a failure.
- Efforts to fix and change things by performance & perfectionism. (It's up to me.)
- Handling all the injustices. (It's not fair, I'm mad, I'm depressed, I give up.)

Fathers are supposed to:

- Affirm and validate the value and worth of their child.
- Offer primary life supports and environmental safety for their child.
- Provide for the emotional stability of their child.
- Provide a protective spiritual and physical covering for their child.
- Provide a spiritual legacy of blessing and a godly inheritance for their child.
- Provide the context for learning for their child.
- Teach and model the behavior of godly choice making, including discipline.
- Define, discover and refine the innate gifts of their child.
- Provide guidance, mentoring, and encouragement and training for their child.
- Provide a financial inheritance for their child.

- Provide a model for learning, love, forgiveness, recovery and fruitfulness.
- Provide the righteous continuation of a godly seed.

BUILDING CONCEPTS

Without fathers, children try to keep themselves safe in shelters made out of scraps of conversation and inconclusive evidence and inadequate explanations about anything. Using their poorly drawn concepts of God, and life, and self, in order to solve heaps of messy problems and unfinished business they rely on nothing but impulse, instinct, and the opinions of others. Many of them must crawl through piles of cruel words and childhood trauma to pull together for themselves a place of safety. Their childish assumptions are all mixed together to form a concept of God, of the world and of themselves. Sadly enough, most of those first ideas do not make sense or work well to solve the next set of issues.

Most of us learn by taking the simpler route of generalization. We reduce our learning time by matching new stuff to old information gathered in similar situations. If a father is a father and all fathers are alike, then all fathers must be like my father, if I have one; and if God is a father, He must be like my father too. So, if my earthly father was easily provoked, absent, angry, busy, or worse yet, harsh and hard to please, then whom do I have in heaven but more of the same? Those raised without a father get to make one up, which could mean God could be anything they want and everything but present.

Anger and depression often set in as secondary responses in these primary relationships creating a permanent feeling of rejection and abandonment, loneliness and helplessness. Hearts are broken and heads become filled with schemes for survival and isolation. Repentance, confession of sin, and forgiveness are not introduced into the place of pain until we are introduced to God. If we are not introduced to the love of God and learn how to forgive, we will stay bound. If we do not know the healing power of His love, our little spirit is left unawakened. We live with our 'spirit candle' unlit (Pr. 20:27) while we sit in the dark and sleep on a bed of despair.

OUR RELATIONSHIP WITH GOD AS A FATHER

In truth, God is the essence of who we are and our relationship with Him will reflect more of His character and attitude the more we come to know Him. The more we know Him, the more we will become like Him. All character changes and attitude adjustments come out of our relationship with God. Our relationship with God begins and ends with Him as our Father. We are his children, called to be His sons and daughters, invited to make our final dwelling place with Him in His home in Heaven.

God has always loved His children and continues to include them in all of His plans, as is evidenced by the fact that He still believes in life and has not stopped creating them, even in the worst of times. Jesus carried on the heart and will of His Father in His kind and inviting response to them. "Then they also brought infants to Him that He might touch them; but when His disciples saw it, they rebuked them. But Jesus called them to Him and said, 'Let the little children come to me, and do not forbid them; for such is the kingdom of God.'" (Lu. 18:15-16)

Jesus includes children of all ages when He speaks of the relationship of an earthly father to that which we have with Him when He said, "If a son asks for bread from any father among you, will he give him a stone? or if he asks for a fish, will he give him a serpent instead of a fish? Or if he asks for an egg, will he offer him a scorpion? If you then, being evil, know how to give good gifts to your children, how much more will your heavenly Father give the Holy Spirit to those who ask Him!" (Mt. 7:9-10)

Jesus is making a strong point here for both compassion and answers to prayer based on the father-child relationship. For most of us that relationship has been a mixed bag with some of us being overprotected and spoiled while others have been starved and neglected. Our relationship with a father has not provided the assurance of our needs getting met or given us the confident peace of knowing that we are heard and loved and cared for.

OBSTACLES WITH OUR FATHER/BROKEN PROMISES

The satisfaction rating of a relationship is based on trust, the ability to produce peace and keep promises. If our perceptions of how well those promises are kept, and our expectations are disregarded and the personal intentions of the other party are misunderstood, trust and reliance will fail. If the One we have trusted in is God, our faith in all God says and has done comes under fire.

Our concept of God comes out of our concept of our father. If our relationship with our father is filled with broken promises, our relationship with God will be subject to disappointment, as well. If our relationship with the man who is supposed to protect and care for us is frustrating, our relationship with our heavenly Father will also be filled with disillusion and hostility. We will have a hard time seeing God as a good and trustworthy father.

Furthermore, if we do not understand the chastening of the Lord, (Heb. 12) we will become bitter and discouraged when our Heavenly Father corrects us. The Enemy is quick to point out how unfair and insensitive God is to our needs. He creates moments or seasons of adversity and uses those vulnerable moments, as he did with Job, to get us to agree with him that we are in pain because God is against us or is punishing us unjustly. If we despise His chastening, the effect of the trial distorts our relationship with Him and can mess up not only our physical bodies, but our relationships with God, as well.

Having a healthy relationship with God as Our Father is not an option if we are to overcome the obstacles we encounter in this life. He desires to provide us with a relationship that protects us and lets us know we are loved and good, and that no matter what it looks like, He has our best interests in mind. If we have a poor relationship or no relationship with Him, we will be rootless and wandering, like wild horses, spooked by fear and defending ourselves from every predator.

Moreover, without a vision, the people perish. They cast off restraint. (See Hos. 4:6) To have no knowledge of God is to reject Him. Having no knowledge leaves us without a sense of origin, or purpose in life, without a reason for being and without direction. If we have no sense of origin, we have no sense of identity or destiny. There will be no accountability, and we will live as ragamuffins and street urchins that belong nowhere and are wanted by no one.

Without someone to love us we feel no purpose, lonely and uncared for. When we feel unloved and see ourselves as unlovable, we become susceptible to sickness and physical and mental break downs. When we do not feel cherished, we do not feel regarded, validated, or justified in our existence. Some conclude that it would have been less painful to not have been given the gift of life in the first place. Self-destruction and hopelessness and negativity overwhelm our souls.

If we have no sense of the value of human life, we will have no sense of dignity nor will the life of any others, including our own, be considered sacred. We will not love, but become lawless, and cold, living wild and frightened, sad and untamed by the love of God.

HINDERED PRAYERS

Raised in this frame of mind, our access to the provision and support of our Heavenly Father is also cut off. Without faith and favor and a good relationship with God as Father, our prayers are hindered and the answers are delayed. Hope diminishes and help does not come. If there is no help, we are stranded on the earth, immersed in despair, and of all men, most miserable.

There will be no communication, no confidence in God's ability to help us or in His willingness to deliver us. There will be no sustaining relationship that will carry us through the hard times. There will be no answers to prayer and our relationships will not be built on faith but failure to believe for the hope of God's comfort.

DISTRUST AND DO IT MYSELF

When our relationships are built on the shallow exchange of information, our feelings about that information become the force that shapes the basis of our relationships, with God, and ourselves, and ultimately, with others. When our relationships are based upon our own feelings and perceptions, our prayers will be lifeless reflections of our own doubt and distrust which will manifest as our need to do it ourselves. When our relationship with God is not based upon the truth of His Word and the sincerity of His promises, we lose confidence in His willingness to help. We have no protection from the predators of Hell.

Loss of confidence in God causes us to turn to ourselves, to supply our own needs, and relying on our own strength. This opens up the door to self-deception and the illusions of self-reliance that lead us away from trusting in and relying on God's leading. Our relationships will be based on selfish ambition, self-seeking, and the fabrication of the truth which makes us susceptible to the lies. If there is no confidence in God or in His authority over the devil and in the extension of His justice to deal justly with the Evil One, we will find no ultimate reason or advantage in having a relationship with God at all.

Our only defense will be our intellect that has already been programmed by the Enemy to reinforce the old messages of self-reliance and false peace. We will be deceived by demons that cleverly disguise themselves as us, as they walk freely in and out of our thoughts and feelings. We will never suspect their impersonations of us as a deadly plot against our souls nor will we resist their ideas in their on-going mischief against us.

We will be overcome and taken up, lost in the lust of the flesh, the lust of the eye, and the pride of life, always wanting the thing we cannot have and trying to get rid of the things we do not want. The vulnerabilities of our flesh, many of which are not bad or evil, but simply legitimate needs, become the open door for the Enemy to pressure us to sin. (See James 1:14-15) When we do not see our needs met by God, or when they are not supplied in a timely fashion, our faith in God is tested, which makes us vulnerable to being enticed by an angel of light who offers a more immediate gratification.

Because we sense no evil or immediate alarm of danger from the temptation, and God's feels remote and uncaring, we are drawn away and enticed into taking the solutions the Tempter offers. We become confused and impatient and step headlong into an agreement with sin. When the sin grows up, the devil calls in the contract we have made with him and death comes in to settle our account. (Ja. 1:14-15)

SUMMARY

If we have a twisted concept of God, Who He is, and what He is like, we will loose our own sense of innate goodness and flounder with issues of morality and righteousness. Our prayers will go unanswered and we will become vulnerable to the temptations of the Evil one. If we see God as an unjust Judge, a universal policeman, or as a greedy landlord, or as non-existent, or unloving, our chances of prevailing against the Enemy of our soul are as good as swimming across the ocean with sand bags on our backs.

Our relationship with God is always a matter of faith and requires much courage in the face of demonic backlash. If we base our relationship on feelings and answers to prayer and not upon His Word, when the answers to prayer are delayed, we become discouraged waiting for God's answer. The Enemy's offer looks more enticing, as a way to eliminate suffering, which seems to be much more of what we wanted. All this makes God look bad and the devil's offer look appealing.

What can go wrong with a father?

- Fear can cause them to abandon, abuse, and neglect their families.
- Failure to provide the covering; instruction, safety and encouragement for their wife and children.
- Take from the child things necessary for him or her to thrive.
- Fathers can deliberately hurt and reject their families, choosing to give themselves to self-indulgent and destructive pursuits.
- They may fail to take leadership and come under the control of a spirit of fear that forces their wives into a position of having to carry the authority in the family.
- They can betray their families into the hands of greed, or lust, where the love of this world and self-ambition carry them away.
- They may still be grappling with their own issues of life, worth, and validity.
- They may pronounce negative words and curses over their child or expose them to emotional and physical dangers.
- They may practice sinful behavior and participate in cult and occult activities that open the door to generational

curses which endanger the spiritual and physical lives of their children.
- They may lose their families through fear of being worthy to be a parent, through divorce, money, sexual perversions, alcoholism, etc.

But the truth is:

- God is none of these! God is love!
- God is the original source of love and the only antidote for fear. (I Jn. 4:16)
- God is our creator. (Gen. 1:1)
- God is our Father. (Mt. 6:9, Mt. 5:16)
- God is the "I AM WHO I AM". (Ex. 3:14)
- God is our Redeemer. (Gal. 3:13)
- God is our deliverer, healer, Savior. (Is. 53:5)
- God is our comforter. (Mt. 11:28-30)
- God is our friend. (Jn. 15:13-15)
- God is our commander-in-chief and captain of the hosts. (Ps. 46:7)
- In Him we abide. (Jn. 15:5)
- In Him all things consist. (Col. 1:15-17)
- In Him we live and move and have our being. (Acts 17:28)
- Through Him we have been translated out of the Kingdom of Darkness into the Kingdom of His Son. (Col. 1:13)

Some Father scriptures for further meditation:

- Psalm 139:1-3 "O LORD, You have searched me and known me. You know my sitting down and my rising up; you understand my thought afar off. You comprehend my path and my lying down, and are acquainted with all my ways."
- Isaiah 64:4-5 "For since the beginning of the world men

have not heard nor perceived by the ear, nor has the eye
seen any God besides You, Who acts for the one who
waits for Him."

- Isaiah 64:8 "But now, O LORD, You are our Father; we are
the clay, and you our potter; and all we are the work of
your hand."
- Isaiah 63:16 "Doubtless, You are our Father, though
Abraham was ignorant of us, and Israel does not
acknowledge us, You, O LORD, are our Father; our
redeemer from Everlasting is Your name."
- Matthew 6:8-13 "Therefore do not be like them. For your
Father knows the things you have need of before you ask
Him. In this manner, therefore, pray: Our Father in
heaven, Hallowed be your name ..."
- I John 2:13 "I write to you, little children, because you
have known the Father."
- Psalm 103:13, "As a father pities his children, so the LORD
pities those who fear Him, for He knows our frame; He
remembers that we are dust."
- Psalm 68:5 "A father of the fatherless, a defender of
widows, is God in His holy habitation. God sets the
solitary in families; He brings out those who are bound
into prosperity; but the rebellious dwell in a dry land."
- Hebrews 12:5-6 "And you have forgotten the exhortation
which speaks to you as to sons; 'My son, do not despise
the chastening of the LORD, nor be discouraged when
you are rebuked by Him; for whom the LORD loves He
chastens and scourges every son whom He receives.'"
- Romans 12:14 "For as many as are led by the Spirit of
God, these are sons of God. For you did not receive the
spirit of bondage again to fear, but you received the Spirit
of adoption by whom we cry out, 'Abba, Father.'"

* * *

CHAPTER 3
MY RELATIONSHIP WITH MYSELF

My relationship with myself becomes the basis for every other relationship I will ever have. All of my thoughts, feelings, perceptions, and experiences form the filters through which I see others. That is why Jesus said to "love your neighbor as yourself". (Mt. 22:39; Mk. 12:31) If I love myself, I will have a place from which to love others. If I hate myself, I will have nothing to give to others, either to comfort or correct them.

The problem is, my first inclinations and perception of 'me', as different and separate from all others, does not come from God. It comes from my perceptions of how others see me. I use their words and responses to build my self-concept. I compare myself to them and judge myself by their expectations even as I begin to embrace their ideas as my own.

The first story of who I am comes out of the story of what happens to me. Like so many other things in life - where one thing depends upon and comes from another - my relationship with myself as seen through the eyes of others becomes an extremely strategic link in the formation of my identity.

If we perceive being 'okay' as being accepted by others or as being able to make them happy with us, we will be locked into an endless cycle of people pleasing, peer pressure and public opinion. If I perceive myself to be 'different' or 'not good enough' or 'less than', I will see myself as 'not okay'. I will subconsciously look for ways to improve my worth and value by looking to others for what I must do to be better and more loved. If I am not secure in who I am, I will be vulnerable to the control of others and their prejudices. Jealousy and cruel words will reign and I will find no place of refuge or protection from their judgment.

The Enemy prefers this type of closed learning system where he controls everything and nothing new, no new information is ever added to the understanding. Controlling everything, including the systems in which we learn things (family, school, etc.) allows him to use fear and intimidation and my motivation to improve myself, to keep the same old responses and reactions in place. Those are the things, learned and relearned, that have been experienced and passed down from one generation to the next.

We are totally unaware of the transmission of generational agreements that establish the pattern of entrapment and enslavement that influence and oppress us. We have been programmed by the 'god of this world' to see life through the lens of our experiences and perceptions. These shape our view of life. Wearing rose colored glasses will color my world pink and perky. Dark lenses paint my world gray and gloomy. How I view myself and my perceptions of what happens to me forms my self-concept. My concept of myself and the world around me colors my world and forms the premise and portal through which all incoming information must flow and be interpreted. My perceptions of what is happening, in turn, form my responses to what is happening.

SELF

And even as my perceptions of the world come out of the perception I have of myself, all of my perceptions I have of myself come out of my perception of how I am perceived by others. This creates a crazy, 'which came first, the chicken or the egg' revolving door that sets up confusion and provides no basis for absolute truth in the formation of who I am. The shifting perceptions, trends and dictates of the 'god of this world' give me no secure or unchanging place in which to anchor my soul or from which I can bring forth a godly response.

The only thing that changes that viscous cycle is to act against the dictates of fear and make a choice to believe the truth of what God says. Because I have a free will and can choose to act out of my soul (flesh) or out of my spirit, even as a follower of Christ, the relationship I have with myself and my view of who I am is still critical to my freedom, and my ensuing ability to influence others for good.

We have been admonished to let our light so shine before men that they may see our good works, peace and joy and love and grace, and glorify our Father who is in Heaven. We communicate about Him through our relationships with others. Knowing the truth about who we are establishes the power of our testimony as witnesses for the God of truth, as well as for the truth of God.

If the system by which my net worth is rendered as flawed and rigged to reduce me to bondage and subject me to condemnation, I will feel like I never measure up. As long as I continue to see myself through the eyes of others they will have the power to define and control me; to promote me or destroy me, to make me mad or glad or sad. This world's system perpetuates the lies and loss of hope from one generation to the next. Sin and iniquity stain our ancestral bloodlines with bloodguilt and push each successive generation further from the truth and into greater relationship deficits

What is the true definition of 'who I am' according to our Creator? God said, in Genesis 1:26-27, "Let Us make man in Our image, according to Our likeness; let them have dominion..." over every other creature. Notice that God never gave this kind of authority or spoke His intention over any of the other creatures, not the fish, or the birds, or the creeping things, or the animals. No other creature, including monkeys, had been given the stamp of God's authentic approval and 'made in His own image and likeness', nor were the other creatures ever given the power to rule over us.

We are special by design. That may be why we gaze so intently at the newborn, still clothed in the holy innocence and purity of heaven. Their countenance is as close to looking into the face of God as anything here on earth. We are amazed to see the signature of God in the detail of their tiny hands and feet. In that moment, we catch a glimpse of our own original divine nature and identity. Hope stirs our hearts and we begin to believe for something better than the brokenness we see all around us in this present evil age.

The revelation of our true worth and value can only be known if we accept our origin as planned and divine. To begin with anything less is to end with tragedy and error. God's Enemy, the devil, is tireless in his efforts to erase and deface God's likeness in us. He hates us. He is driven by that hatred to remove, if possible, God's divine nature and presence from every part of our consciousness awareness. He tricks us into believing that we are the things we see ourselves doing, to get us to agree with him that we are bad and guilty. Many of the things we are deceived into doing are intended to discredit and reject the divine nature of God in us and lead us to embrace a theology of the depravity of man and a doctrine of good works.

FORMING MY SELF-CONCEPT

In our natural mind, we use the things we see ourselves doing, to form our self-concept. Analyzing our behavior and using the things we learned provides us with the information we need to help us respond to the next set of events. Using the things we learned in the last situation, we begin to form our sense of 'self' and our strategies for safety. Building our self-concept based on what we see ourselves doing allows the spirit of fear to both solidify my concept of who I am and dictate future responses to the events to keep bad things from happening again. The Enemy is using fear as a negative reinforcement to program my behavior.

I determine my worth:

- By what other people say about me.
- By what other people do to me.
- By what happens to me.
- By how I feel and think about what has happened to me.
- By how I feel and think about what I perceive has happened to me.
- By what I see myself doing, saying, thinking and feeling.
- By what God's Word says about me.

Most of us, at the beginning of our lives give little thought to analyzing any of what happens to us in the light and counsel of God's Word. We are stuck using the first six ways of gathering and evaluating the information to determine our worth. Use this inventory to get a clearer understanding of how you see yourself.

MY SELF PROFILE

How would you answer these questions?

- Write four words that others would/have used to describe you.
- Write four words that <u>you</u> would use to describe yourself.
- Write four words you would use to describe your relationship with someone you are close to.
- Write four words you would use to describe your relationship with God.
- I am _____(fill in the blank with the first words that come to your mind).

- How would you describe your childhood in three to ten words?
- Do you like yourself? Are you happy with who you are?
- Do you compare yourself with others and wish you were like them? How?
- What would you like to change about yourself, if anything?
- What have you tried to change about yourself? Have you succeeded?
- What have you given up on changing about yourself?
- Did Jesus Christ actually tell us to be good, make better choices, or change?
- How would you describe someone who was their own worst enemy? Did you just describe yourself?
- Are you hard on yourself? Why would you do that?
- How does setting you up in opposition to yourself profit the Kingdom of God?
- Do you believe everything you tell yourself?
- Do you believe everything others tell you about yourself?
- Do you think every thought or feeling that you think or feel are your own thoughts or feelings?
- When you see yourself misbehaving do you ever wonder who is 'acting up' in there? (Rom. 7:20)
- When I'm 'out of control', and doing the thing I'm trying not to do, who is in control of my life at that moment? (Rom.7:15) Be honest with yourself.
- Who is saying some of the things that come out of my mouth that I am ashamed of? (Rom. 7:17)

ENVIRONMENTAL BOX INVENTORY

DIRECTIONS: Answer as specifically as you can – avoid the non-committal answers like "I don't know". (Be honest - this is for you).

- My life growing up was____. (use your own words)
- My childhood could best be described as_____.
- Was the answer to the last question accurate? Or did you describe your pretend world?

Parents

- Four words that I would use to describe my mother.
- Four words that I would use to describe my Father.
- I was expected to, (obey, raise my siblings, make my parents feel better, be seen and not heard), growing up.
- Four words that would describe my parent's marriage(s).
- I was _____ (use your own words) growing up.
- Our house was (neat, chaotic, fun, scary, perfect, other).

Activities/Roles

- My family (never, always, sometimes) did things together. What things?
- My job in the family was to_____.
- I learned to (hide, get attention, comply, be silent, take charge, do my part, expect nothing, ask for help, do it myself, other), in my family.
- I had a curfew.
- I had chores. (Name some)

School

- School was _____.
- I did well/bad in school.
- _____was my worst subject.
- _____was my favorite subject.
- Friends were _____.
- I liked to _____ when I was young.
- I had (no, few, lots of, other), friends at school.

- There was abuse, (what kind?) _____ in our family.

God

- God was (important, irrelevant, other) in our family.
- Church was _____.

Food/Eating

- Mealtime was _____.
- Dad would _____ at the table.
- Mom would _____ at the table.
- Food is _____
- We eat food to _____.
- Food was, (never an issue for me, the source of love and comfort, a sign of love, about dieting) _____.
- I ate, (what I was told, what was put on my plate, what I liked, what I wanted, when I wanted, at meal time as a family, by myself, other)_____.
- I had trouble with eating food because _____.

Self Image

- I like how I look. I like my_____.
- I don't like my _____.
- I wish I could change _____ about my life.
- I got teased for _____.
- I grew up (liking, hating, not liking, confused about) myself.

CITY-SOUL

The Bible describes us as a 'city-soul'. "And they shall rebuild the old ruins, they shall raise up the former desolations, and they shall repair the ruined cities, the desolations of many generations." (Is. 61:4) "Violence shall no longer be heard in your land, neither wasting nor destruction within your borders; but you shall call your wall Salvation, and your gates Praise." (Is. 60:18)

Our city-souls have been invaded. Though we do not initially comprehend the danger of that invasion, we are, nonetheless, being gradually and systematically overcome by the lies of the Snake Pit. At the moment of our conception we were plunged into that Pit where Satan, the 'god of this world' began to psychologically recondition us to obscure our divine nature and convince us that we have a sinful human nature which we must overcome to get to Heaven. We have been programmed by the things we see and hear and feel and taste (Reality), to believe what things 'look like' more than what God's Word has to say about them.

Satan and his world are at enmity with God and are contrary to His divine nature in us. He uses a 'divide and conquer' strategy to set us up in opposition to ourselves, (II Tim. 2:25) to make desolate the Kingdom of God that resides within us. This is the same strategy he has used from the beginning to bring destruction to our first parents and divide their relationship with God's who desires to dwell in the midst of us. (Mt. 12:29 and Lu. 11:17-28)

Most people consider Satan's spiritual agenda to destroy them as farfetched, something only a 'fanatic follower' of Jesus Christ would believe. The idea of the spiritual take-over of an individual soul is thought to be 'small potatoes' for one so intent upon the ruling the world as Satan. But how else would one conquer the world except through conquering it, one kingdom at a time. We are all little kingdoms, each part of the greater Kingdom of God.

The devil's simple 'tried and true strategy' of deception to divide, and conquer each kingdom by isolating each one from the love and support of the other, still works well. How better to accomplish the feat and our secure our defeat than to make us too busy or distracted to war against darkness or keep a watchful eye on the wall, or walk in the victory already provided for us?

DIVISIBLE AND SET UP IN OPPOSITION TO MY OWN SELF

II Timothy gives a very succinct summary of Satan's work among us in his admonition to the servants of the Lord. He tells them that they must be "gentle to all, able to teach, patient, in humility correcting those who are in opposition to themselves, (KJV), if God perhaps will grant them repentance, (the grace to change their mind and stop believing the lie) so that they may KNOW the truth, and that they may come to their senses and escape the snare of the devil, having been taken captive by him to do his will." (II Tim. 2:24-26)

Satan takes every opportunity to try and convince me I am bad. Through accusation and the commission of sin he convinces me I am the evil I hate. If I am the sin I hate, then to get rid of the sin I hate, I must get rid of myself. Satan's solution to my sin is for me to get rid of myself. With my agreement, the spirit of self-destruction begins to tear away my sense of justice and goodness in hopes of using me to destroy myself. How clever is that?

WHAT HINDERS ME FROM KNOWING WHO I AM?

One of the most misunderstood and misdirected efforts in this war for truth begins with the Enemy trying to set me up in 'opposition to myself'. This allows him to justify his criminal assaults against me because 'I have agreed to it'. When I agree with his desire to erase my divine nature and re-write it as a sinful human nature, I have surrendered my options of knowing the truth about who I am and my relationship with my heavenly Father, to the lie.

God's image and likeness are contained within us. What other pastime would be more worthy of Satan's attention and effort than to corrupt the image of God we carry within us? If the same basic strategy of divide and conquer used in war in the natural can be applied to the war we experience in our souls, then before the devil can divide that which was made indivisible, he must deceive us into believing we are not already complete. To make that agreement with ourselves, we must be already compromised into believing we are missing something, just like the Enemy did with Eve.

The Enemy's strategy begins with tempting us to believe a lie. We believe the lie and we sin. Satan then uses our sin to convince us that we are bad. We then get all tangled up in trying to prove him wrong by trying harder to be good, only to fail and end up running out of ways to defend ourselves. He uses the very acts he has tempted us into doing in the first place, as evidence to prove that we are 'not good'. Our case seems hopeless. We settle into believing that we are what we do, and when we see ourselves doing hateful things, we conclude we must be a horrible person. (Rom. 7:15-25)

The Word of God offers three solutions to this human dilemma. The first is to die to the old nature, the carnal man and let him be crucified with Christ. The second is to forget those things that are behind. Let go of the past and refuse to let the past determine our future. We need to forgive ourselves and confess our sins to Him Who is Faithful and Just to "forgive us our sins and cleanse us from all unrighteousness". (I Jn. 1:8) And third, we let Jesus be our advocate, our defense attorney. We rest our hope in Him as He presents our case before the Court of Heaven.

BORN INTO THE SNAKE PIT

We are born into captivity. We are born into the Snake Pit of this world system and enslaved by the god of this world. We are enslaved by sin, not depraved. As slaves, even before we entered into his domain, Satan had begun to work in us and in our generations to set us up for destruction. The rule of law in this world is 'you are what you do'. If Satan, through his lies can get us to believe we are what we do, he can torment us with endless accusations.

He tempts our souls, (our mind, will and emotions), with both fear and desire, in order to put us on the torture racks of Hell. We end up being torn apart 'trying to quit what we cannot stop', in order to convince ourselves we are not who the devil says we are. He wants us to agree that we are not worth anything and if we are to be considered worth anything, we must prove it first.

HELLS TEACHERS

We have been raised in Hell's schoolhouse. Its lessons are taught by Reality, Religion, Responsibility and Reasoning - the four R's from hell. As we learn the lessons of life under the unforgiving eye of the Evil One and the endless taunting of 'should have, could have, it's my fault, and try harder', we are drawn further away from God and the truth of who we are.

If the first lessons we are taught about our identity are learned in Hell's classrooms taught by the counselors of Hell, we will be easily defeated. Once we are convinced that we are bad because we do bad things, we are defenseless. Once we are convinced 'we are what we do', our souls have been over taken by fear. We are captured and brainwashed before we even realize there is a war going on.

How fair is that? In truth, it is not! But that does not stop the devil from moving forward. He makes no apology for 'not being fair' or wanting to destroy the children of God. He makes no exceptions for ignorance. We are no match for him or his clever plans. If I take on this war as a personal fight when I am already held as a his prisoner, I will come under the delusion that I can save myself. We are no match for the wiles of the god of this world. We must surrender our position to God and He will save us!

My righteousness was lost when the devil tried to stripe me of my divine nature and remake me in his image as one of the sons of Hell. I am captured and held by the power of the lie when I believe that God's goodness has departed from me and His image no longer rests in me. I am deceived and held hostage when the Enemy uses my desire to prove I am righteous apart from God's righteousness.

If I believe what the Word of God says, and walk, "not by sight, but by faith," (II Cor. 5:7) I will walk in the truth and in the freedom it brings. Though I have no righteousness apart from the Lord Jesus Christ and no way to obtain it within myself, I do have an opportunity for that righteousness to be restored. The Lord has come to reestablish us in our right mind and in our rightful inheritance through the Atonement He made for us on the Cross. His death satisfied the demands death had made upon us and paid the ransom for my soul. My new life and legacy is based upon my identity as being one of the sons or daughters of God, not on anything I do. Through adoption, I have been translated out of the Kingdom of Darkness into the Kingdom of Light and restored me as a legitimate heir to eternal life.

God has given each of us the opportunity to be 'bought back' through His Blood into His Kingdom through our acceptance of His substitutionary death for our sins. When I choose to believe the truth of Who I was created BY, I can receive the truth of who I am created to BE. When I submit to the truth of God, that I am His, my identity becomes established in my origin and I can say, like Jesus, 'I know who I am because I know where I came from'. (Jn. 7:28 & Jn. 8:14)

FORGIVING MYSELF AND FORGETTING THE PAST

Because we develop our original self-concept from the things we do, and the things we see laying around us, a lot of what we have to work with in constructing our life concepts, including the concept of 'self' is junk. Sin, failure, fear, and an endless list of other things we are ashamed of get knit into the fabric of who we are. Our own sense of failed expectations and shortcomings builds a case in our minds against any hope of our returning to our original innate goodness. Our frustrated efforts to 'be good,' along with everyone else's ideas of how that goodness should look leave us in serious need of self-forgiveness by the time we are five.

The Enemy is the originator of that frustration. As the accuser of the brethren, he convinces and constantly reminds us of our failures using our own thoughts and feelings to hold us in judgment and unforgiveness against ourselves. He reminds us of wrongs and offenses that we have both committed and have suffered.

These records of wrongs, both those that were done to us and the ones we did to others, mix with unanswered prayers to create a bitter hedge of offense between us and ourselves, others and between us and God. If my relationship between me and myself is filled with self-bitterness, my relationship with God will taste bitter, as well. My relationship with Him will not be one of sweet communion, but of alienation and fear and distrust.

That is why forgiveness and self-forgiveness - releasing myself from the judgments I've made against myself - are essential in not only embracing my true identity and worth, but in healing other relationships, as well. If it is true that most of what we learned and came to believe about ourselves and others growing up were lies, then the most important part of life after childhood is unlearning those lies and forgiving those we judged for practicing them.

Concepts and belief systems and conclusions regarding anything that was made obtained using our mind or our heart and based on our experience is subject to grave and serious error. If we hold on to those ideas as true and elevate them to the place of truth when, in fact, they were lies, they will bind and destroy us. If the thing we believe to be true is not the Truth, "how great is that darkness" Jesus said. (Mt. 6:23)

If most of our walk as a believer in Jesus Christ is about unlearning the things we learned; then we must become comfortable letting go of the things we had become so familiar with and had come to believe were the truth. We must identify the source of truth knowing its stability will not change with time or be altered by the opinions of others.

The Word of God is the truth and holds the final word on who I am. In adding up the sum of all the things that have happened to us it admonishes us to 'forget' or let go of, "those things that are behind and reaching forward to those things which are ahead", to "press toward the goal for the prize of the upward call of God in Christ Jesus." (Phil. 3:13-14)

THE REVELATION OF JESUS CHRIST

The most important antidote to the poison of lie is to know the truth about Who Jesus is. He is the light Who gives true insight into who I am.

Obstruction to His light comes through:

- Preoccupation with myself, either my sin or my own goodness. (Lk. 8:18)
- Preoccupation with the sins others have committed, against me, or others. (Mt. 18:18)
- Pursuit of my own goodness. (Lk. 18:18)
- Pursuit of riches, personal safety and gain. (Lk. 18:22)
- Preconceived ideas of how things should be. (Lk. 18:31)
- Putting the crown before the cross. (Mt. 16:26)
- Personal hardship and spiritual blindness. (Lk. 18:35)
- Other obstacles you have encountered to humbling yourself to walk in the truth. (Ja. 5:16)

Examine your own thoughts. What are some of the lies you need to unlearn?

THE TAKEOVER

Ephesians describes the spiritual war between God and Satan for the souls of men by reminding us that we do not "wrestle against flesh and blood, but against principalities, against powers, against the rulers of the darkness of this age, against spiritual hosts of wickedness in the heavenly places". (Eph. 6:12) Jesus personalized that battle and the Enemy even more when He told us about the 'stronger man' in Mt. 12:29 and Lu. 11:21-22, that has come to "plunder" our house.

"When a strongman, fully armed, guards his own palace, his goods are in peace. But when a stronger than he comes upon him and overcomes him, he takes from him all his armor in which he trusted, and divides his spoils". (Lu. 11:21-22)

If the one who comes to "plunder the house" is driven out, Jesus warns us, he will consult with other spirits, more wicked than himself, and form some kind of demonic alliance to construct a plan to get back in. He "takes with him seven other spirits more wicked than himself, and they enter and dwell there; and the last state of that man is worse than the first." (Lu. 24-26) This would lead us to believe there is a demonic strategy and intelligence that has the ability to plot against our lives with deliberate and 'thought out' intention.

If this is true, the battle is real and Satan's agenda is specific. He sets up his opposition to twists things around to take me out. He begins to divide and conquer my house by causing me to doubt my own intentions and question my actions. He wants me to see myself as stupid and my actions as sin.

Speaking in the 'first person' he whispers his thoughts into my mind, mingling my thoughts with his until I cannot discern the difference. 'It's my fault. I did it. And it was my idea', are all part of the case he makes against my soul to get me to take the blame for what I did and see myself as the sin I committed. I told a lie. It was my mouth that did it. Because I cannot deny or refute that 'fact,' Satan's claim appears to be the 'truth.' I become the first one to be persuaded that the things he says about me are correct and I am guilty.

DISCERNING AND DISSECTING YOUR OWN THOUGHTS

The Enemy's demonic programming is so embedded within us - described by Paul as the "body of death" (Rom. 7:24) "warring against the law of my mind," (Rom. 7:23) that we have become conditioned by the Evil One to believe that his thoughts are our own. He has become so familiar to us that his influence and activities are no longer discerned as different from ours. Because his voice comes to us as our own, we must be determined to make a more diligent effort to heed the Holy Spirit to "take captive every thought, and make it subject to the obedience of Christ." (II Cor. 10:5)

The Bible says, "What the heart is full of the mouth speaks". (Mt. 12:34) This makes the mouth an accurate representation of what is going on in our hearts, and an incredibly helpful method of discerning the thoughts and intentions of our hearts. Unless we listen to what is coming out of our mouth and honestly consider those words, we will not be able to recognize or be aware of the insidious, demonic treachery and control the Enemy has over us in manipulating what is going on inside of us.

If the words that are coming out of our mouth are not words from God or the counsel of the Holy Spirit that lives inside of us, we know we are being 'hacked into' by the Enemy. What goes on inside of us at a deep sub-conscious level, or even at a conscious level, is not always apparent to us, however. We have become 'used to' the stream of consciousness and 'self-talk' that we hear coming out of our mouths.

We have become so familiar with our thoughts and words and the behavior that follows that we rarely question what we are thinking or ponder where those thoughts and feelings are coming from. We simply accept our thoughts and act on our feelings. We see them as a legitimate expression of ourselves and 'go along with' whatever it is we are thinking or feeling, or hear ourselves saying to ourselves. The Enemy has counterfeited our thoughts and fed them back to us as our own.

If you assume your 'Self-talk' is you talking to yourself, think again. <u>Not every thought you think you thought are thoughts you thought. Some of the thoughts you think you thought are thoughts the Enemy wants you to think you thought, so he can get you to accept them as your own.</u>

What are some of the things you have heard yourself saying today about yourself? What did you hear yourself saying about your spouse, boss, parent, other people? What have you heard yourself thinking and saying about God?

Now, ask yourself, are those thoughts from Heaven, or from Hell? (See Mt. 21:25) Do they bring joy and peace or stress and confusion? Rendering the thoughts or reducing them 'down' to their lowest common denominator, like we do in math, will reveal which kingdom they are from, Heaven or Hell. Jesus told us that, "by their fruits we will know them," (Mt. 7:20) therefore, this simple exercise should not be that hard!

HEARING VOICES

Schizophrenia is a diagnosis that describes the experiences of someone who is hearing or thinks they are hearing 'voices in their head'. Some assume if someone is hearing voices in their head, they are crazy. The simple truth is that they are hearing voices of other entities, better known as demons or evil spirits. These voices are coming from beings that are conversing either with us or about us in our presence.

The things they are speaking about to each other, or directly to you, are NOT your thoughts. The manifestations or experience of 'hearing voices' indicates you have been programmed, more or less, invaded by the demonic entities to drive you crazy. They are the forces behind cutting, self-sabotage, self-destruction, suicide and suicidal behavior. It is important to remember that these voices ARE NOT YOU! They are using your mind, will, and emotions to get control of your body, to pursue their own agenda which is to destroy you. The remedy for such situations is deliverance which means we submit to God, resist the devil and he will flee. The Enemy is claiming a right in your life that he acquired through the sin of your generation. If you are a Believer in Jesus Christ, the Enemy's legal claim to that right has been broken through the Blood of Jesus Christ. God wants you and your team of fellow believers to enforce that freedom and join together in commanding the spirits to leave. Deliverance is the real solution to any and all of the mental illnesses diseases.

Though some may hear these voices regularly or others, only on occasion, because they are very disturbing, many go on an anti-psychotic medication to silence them. None of these medications have the power to deliver you from these spirits. All they do is create adverse chemical reactions in your already distressed biological systems and create more negative side effects. Anti-psychotic medications may be a temporary help to mask the symptoms but are no remedy for bizarre behavior of demonic spirits. They are like using a crutch for a broken leg. Even as the crutch cannot heal the broken leg, neither can these meds solve the problem of mental illness. All they do is isolate you even more from the fellowship of others through confusion and create complicated side effects that make you feel like you are crazy.

In the paradigm of modern world thinking, demons do not exist and therefore cannot be included in the explanation of anything alien or paranormal. Anyone who believes in spiritual warfare or the existence of an unseen world is labeled a crazy, conspiracy theorist or unscientific. This makes it difficult to find help in the medical community as a whole. People who are missing the spiritual factor of 'evil' in the equation they are using to try and figure out what is going on in the world miss the obvious. They usually fall back on labeling those plagued with these kind spiritual attacks against the mind and emotions and insist on putting them on medications to quiet the voices.

Paul clearly made it a matter of 'deliverance' when he cried out, "Oh wretched man that I am, who will deliver me from this body of death?" (Rom. 7:24) Even if you have become so used to hearing them 'talking with you' that you think nothing of it, and you feel 'they' are helpful in keeping you company, allowing these 'visitors' to become permanent residents of your house and head is not wise or advisable.

Some call these demonic entities 'spirit guides', their personal 'angel' or their 'imaginary friends'. They look to them as protectors, and allow them to channel through them or reveal to them secret things, hidden mysteries, and forbidden knowledge. These voices are not the Holy Spirit that has been sent to lead us and guide us into all truth (Jn. 16:13) but anti-christ spirits, false Jesuses and spirits of divination.

If the voices speaking to you, either audibly or as a strong suggestion, are craving or fear they are not from Heaven. If you have been 'saved' through confession in the Jesus Christ as your Savior, they have NO right to be in your temple, because you are the temple property of the Most High God! They have no right to act as your advisory council or as spiritual scorekeepers. As saved, Blood bought sons and daughters of our Father, Who is God, the Kingdom of Darkness has no more right to anything that belongs to us and has been given to us by our Father.

To end the discussion, and silence these voices we must recognize they are not us. We must submit to God, resist the devil (Ja. 4:7) and command them to leave our house. Casting them out occurs only when these spirits are commanded to leave. They have been 'invited' through past agreements and generational iniquities that have not been dealt with. You may not realize or remember when that invitation was given or the curse came, but to effectively get rid of them, you must 'cancel out' the agreements you and your ancestors made with them.

The invitations they are using to continue their occupation of the house may be centuries old. And because they have been made in the past, you may not even be aware of them. You may think they have nothing to do with you, but that does not make the Enemy leave. The authority of your command in the Name of Jesus Christ gained through confession of the sins of the fathers and repentance for your participation in them, both knowingly and unknowingly, gives you the right to command them to leave.

Sin and iniquity, and the trauma that accompanied the initial assault and the crimes that came as against our lives as a result of those injustices are marked on our DNA. The DNA provide the codes and become the information site the Enemy uses to mark the areas he has gained access to through the agreements with iniquity. These old agreement made by our ancestors have given him permission to carry their sin of idolatry and fear down into our lives. He uses those agreements to control certain parts of our lives and activities and build his case against us in the Court of Heaven. He is determined to use the unconfessed sin of the past to pursue his right to control us.

If he can continue to occupy and control the 'temple of God', even though he no longer owns us, or has a 'legal' right to us, he will. Just because there is a law against robbing the bank doesn't mean the bank robbers stop robbing banks. Just because our past is 'under the Blood' and our sins are forgiven does not mean the Enemy won't try to challenge our faith in the finished work of

Jesus Christ. He will continue to subdue and enslave us, even after we are saved, if he can get us to go along with it. That is why even 'saved people' have so much trouble in relationships.

THOUGHT INVENTORY

'Hearing voices' in your head talking with you is not the same as 'talking out loud to yourself.' The first is a group of familiar spirits who would like to monitor and mentor and decide for you, what to do, or how well you did, or what you need to do better or different next time. The second is simply a way of staying on track and concentrating.

Identify which of the following statements are thoughts that form the background 'noise' you live with daily? The 'background noise' forms the general disposition of your soul, (mind, will, and emotion) which we could also define as 'the self'. Feelings emanate from the heart which is part of the soul. Thoughts come from the mind. Both are part of our soul. Our body and soul together define the 'flesh'. When the body and soul are connected we are alive. When they disconnect, we die.

When we are 'walking in the flesh' our emotions and our thoughts control our words and actions. When our words and actions that come from our 'flesh' and not from our 'spirit' determine our relationships, the quality of the communication in those relationships will be unstable and difficult. This is because the things that originate in our hearts and minds and processed through our wills are subject to demonic influences and even control.

Check to identify those thoughts and feelings that run in the background of your soul. You may rate them as; frequent (3), sometimes (2), hardly ever (1), never, (0). Add up your score.

Positives

- Nothing is impossible with God.
- I can do all things through Christ.
- It's going to be all right.
- I can do it.
- Thank you!
- God is good.
- You did a great job.
- God is with me.
- I forgive you.
- We can do it.
- I knew we could do it.
- Never give up.
- It's going to be okay.

Anything above 35 is Great! When we are thinking on what so ever things are pure, lovely, honest, just and of good report, (Phil. 4:8) we are keeping our mind stayed on Christ and developing a permanent anchor of hope in our long term memory. Congratulations!!

Rate yourself the same way for this list:

Negatives

- It's too hard. I can't do it.
- What's the use? I give up. I quit.
- I should have. I need to_____.
- It's my fault. It's not my fault. It's their fault.
- If only, _____.
- It's too late.
- It's never enough. It's never good enough.
- No one likes me.
- No one ever listens to me.
- I don't know. I don't get it.
- Whatever! I don't care.
- You can't make me. Don't tell me what to do.

- I want it now. I can't wait.
- You don't understand.
- No one loves me. No one cares about me.
- I don't have a choice.
- It's not fair! It never works for me!
- I knew it would never work.

The total possible worst score is 54. The lower your score, the better. Keep your mind stayed on Christ! You are defeating the giant of pessimism and murmuring and becoming a more pleasant person to be around.

The strategy of our Enemy has always been to "divide our house" and "set us up in opposition to ourselves." (II Tim. 2:25 KJV) How does being your own 'worst enemy' profit the Kingdom of God? It does not! Negative speaking, however, does profit the Kingdom of Darkness and allows the 'stronger man' to come in and steal our weapons and plunder our house, all of which, promotes the destruction of our house and our testimony.

ABIDE OR HIDE

We are no longer strangers to God or enemies of the Cross. As the Holy Spirit continues to lead us into all truth (Jn. 16:13) God perfects "that which concerns us" (Ps. 138:8) As I follow Him, I join with Him in carrying out the Great Commission. The work is to believe in Him; to know that "to live is Christ" (Phil. 1:21) and it is "Christ in you, the hope of glory," (Col. 1:27) because it is "Christ Who is our life" (Col. 1:3) and therefore, "In Him we live and move and have our being". (Acts 17:28)

Our new position and relationship in Christ is to be that of a branch to a vine. As the branch "abides in the vine" (Jn. 15:5) we too are grafted into Christ. We now take our sustenance and strength from Him. Our identity is in Him. Our position is in Him. He is our Savior. He is our righteousness. He is our faithful witness. The three core issues of life, safety, righteousness, and whose responsibility is it are all solved in the love of Jesus Christ for us.

Through the work of the Cross He has created a way for us to be grafted into Him and to return to our original nature, which is our divine nature, created to be His son or His daughter. The rest of our life on earth then, becomes one of abiding in the Vine and allowing Him to live His life through us which allows us to bring forth fruit that will remain.

CHAPTER 4
MY RELATIONSHIP WITH SIN

We cannot speak but a few sentences about 'man' before we must address the issue of sin. No discussion of human relationships can be complete without its inclusion, even as human life and experience cannot be fully described outside of the context of it.

Sin is all around us, like the air we breathe. It taints the color of our world with a dirty scummy gray that diminishes life's luster with guilt and despair. Sin is the transgression of the law. It is anything that we do or say or meditate upon that separates us from the love of God, others or ourselves

Since 'the fall,' sin and getting rid of it, have become the biggest preoccupation of the human race and Satan's greatest windfall opportunity. The "wages of sin is death." (Rom. 6:23) Death is ultimate separation from God forever. Our relationship with sin therefore, determines our relationship with God and our eternal destiny. If we hate sin and flee from it we will be preserved. If we fall into it and do not repent, change our mind and turn from it, we will die.

Remember: there are many forms and practices of sin that do not at first appear sinful or wrong, or deadly. Examples of these kinds of sin include; worry, denial, murmuring, ingratitude, self-reliance, self-indulgence, doubt, criticizing, minimizing sin, excuse making, coldness, isolation, indifference, apathy, religious practices, and substitution of our own works for surrender to God.

Our relationship with God has been greatly affected by sin. Nothing is the way it first was when Adam and Eve finished off their day by walking with God. Now we live lost, in the heat of the night and in the storms of life. Through Isaiah God pleads with us, "Come now, and let us reason together, says the LORD, though your sins are like scarlet, they shall be as white as snow, though they are red like crimson, they shall be as wool. If you are willing and obedient, you shall eat the good of the land; but if you refuse and rebel, you shall be devoured by the sword." (Is. 1:18-20)

SINS OF OMISSION, COMMISSION, ASSUMPTION, AND PRESUMPTION

Sins of Omission are things we fail or refuse to do, both knowingly and ignorantly. Jesus scolded the Pharisees for failing to continue to honor their parents by giving their gifts to the temple instead. Using their giving to the temple as an excuse to neglect their parents was not God's idea of right relationships. "Pure and undefiled religion, before God and the Father is this: to visit orphans and widows in their trouble, and to keep oneself unspotted from the world," (Ja. 1:27) a far cry from what the religious leaders of His day were teaching.

Sins of Commission are acts done in direct violation of the Ten Commandments. They may be deliberate and willful or things done under coercion and out of fear. They can be overt or covert as Jesus equates looking at a woman and lusting in your heart for her is the same as doing the deed. (Mt. 5:28)

Sins of Assumption, include the more subtle work of darkness that would make us think we are believing the truth when, in fact, we are making an assumption that we are abiding in the truth when we are not. Trying to be good implies we are not good and or not good enough. This opens the door for condemnation and strife, which stresses us out and cause us to depart from the 'rest' and trust in God, which is most definitely part of the will of God for us. It also provokes us to do 'religious' deeds that cannot fulfill the requirements of the law or make us holy.

Sins of Presumption are those we commit when we do not know our place. We are blinded to the truth and we are persuaded that we are exempt from God's commandments and can break God's laws of love and divine authority to bring justice ourselves. David prayed that God would keep him from presumptuous sins like touching God's anointed. Even when Saul, his king and the one God had anointed to lead the people, was clearly out of order, David knew his place and let the correction be God's not his.

Many are tempted to bring divine order and do God's bidding by fighting 'holy' wars that become nothing but an opportunity for the Devil to shed innocent blood and exalt folly. Jesus so rightly prophesied, "They will kill you and think they have done God a service". (Jn. 16:2) Or they get caught up in 'playing the Holy Spirit' in other people's lives and end up judging others and justifying themselves, neither of which leads to godliness.

SIN BREAKS THE LAW OF LOVE

All sin, however it may be categorized, fails to walk out God's commandment to love, which is ultimately what makes sin sinful. Sin separates us from God Who is love and causes us to transgress against the law of love. Love ignites passion and incites compassion to care for others. When lawlessness abounds love grows cold. (Mt. 24:12)

Sin begins with two things, need and the temptation to fill that need outside of God's provision. Temptation is the Enemy's solution to our need. The flesh has needs and vulnerabilities. Those needs make it weak and susceptible to demonic suggestion. Being weak does not make us or our flesh evil. "For I know that in me, (that is, in my flesh) nothing good <u>dwells</u>." (Rom. 7:18) It does, however, make us an easy target for the tempter.

The Greek word for flesh is 'sarx'. The flesh as defined and used in the Bible has many different meanings but all written with the same word, 'sarx'. The true meaning then, must be derived from the context in which the word is used. Three of them include, "the weaker element in human nature", "the unregenerate state of man" and "the seat of sin in man, which is not the same as the body". See Vine's Expository Dictionary of New Testament Words, pg.107-108.

HUMAN VULNERABILITY

The flesh, in itself, is NOT evil. "It is fearfully and wonderfully made", (Ps. 139:14) but through need, it has becomes vulnerable to evil. Our need for love and affirmation, and safety; the need for recognition and to be valued are God given. He intends to fill those needs Himself. Satan, however, sees these needs as his golden opportunity to answer our 'prayers' and so, tempts us to take his offer, always a close counterfeit of the truth, but set up to destroy us.

Satan's solutions are often disguised to look like 'the will of God' or like 'taking responsibility' for ourselves. Many of these pious looking suggestions are nothing more than a cheap trick to get us to trust in ourselves, or listen to fear. Once we take the Enemy's solution, condemnation moves in to bring shame which pressures us to take on the guilt that rightly belongs to the Enemy. When we accept the Devil's provision instead of God's we become obligated to him.

Sin is a personal matter and must be dealt with personally. We cannot delegate anyone else to do our repentance or confession for us. God's provision and reconciliation has been extended to each of us, but the response is ours. He has given us the freedom to live as we like, but not without consequences. He makes no exceptions to His impartiality and does not respect us with differing degrees of preference. The choice, whether to trust Him or the Enemy is ours

God's suffering as a result of us using our free will and choice to sin is incalculable. The amount of pain and injustice our choices unleashes in the lives of others, many of whom are His innocent children, must be incredible. As a Father, God has to feel it. He knows all of it. And, according to His word, He must endure it until the cup of His wrath is full and judgment spills out. Many of us judge God as too tolerant or indifferent to our pain. We criticize His patience as injustice at the same time we condemn Him for His judgments.

The only way we can truly appreciate His position is if we are allowed to "enter into the fellowship of His suffering", (Phil. 3:10). That often happens when we suffer at the hands of our own children as they rebel against us, distrust us, criticize us, reject our advice and break our hearts with their foolish and insensitive insults against our good intentions toward them. Just as their rejection of us separates us from them, our sin against God is an insult to His goodness and love - the One Who bled and died for us that we might live. His forgiveness is truly as amazing as His love.

WHY DO I SIN?

Sin entered into 'Act One' of the human drama and has been with us ever since. If "all have sinned and fallen short of the glory of God" (Rom. 3:23) - and we have - and if, "In my flesh dwells no good thing," then the question becomes not, 'will' we sin, BUT, 'when' we sin and 'why'. How does sin affect us? All of us have broken at least one of the Ten Commandments. So, does that make us depraved or does that make us enslaved and deceived?

If I am defined by what I do, then 'doing sins' makes me a sinner. (In Greek, however, 'sinner' is an adjective not a noun. An adjective DESCRIBES something about a person, place or thing, what they do, or their attributes. The adjective 'sinner' is properly used to describe someone who does 'sins'. A subject, on the other hand, NAMES a person, place or the thing. The real question is how does God define me? Does He define me by what I do, or by who I am? Does what I do change who I am? Can I still be the son or daughter of God if I sin? Can I still be the daughter of my father if I rob the bank (sin)? Of course!

But, if I am already depraved – that is, I am already vile and evil - why would Satan continue to hate me so much and try to destroy the image of God in me so completely? Why would he seek to corrupt what is already corrupt and persuade us to leave God if we were already sons of hell? Also consider this: if we were born depraved; we would be of the devil. If we were of the devil, we would have no desire for righteousness nor would we feel bad or guilty when we sin.

If we are of God, however, and listen to a lie, and believe that lie enough to act upon it, we will sin. When we sin, we are bound by the lie and taken captive by Satan. We become "slaves of sin" (Jn. 8:34) "Do you not know that to whom you present yourselves slaves to obey, you are that one's slave whom you obey, whether of sin to death or of obedience to righteousness?" (Rom. 6:16) Jesus told us, "Whoever commits sin is a slave of sin." (Jn. 8:34)

So, what about sin? Does the presence of 'sin' in our lives prove we are depraved, or prove that we are weak and vulnerable to being deceived by the devil? And could part of the original deception be to create a theology that pushes us into embracing our propensity to sin as proof of that depravity which further pushes us into believing we are born bad and unloved by God?

What a brilliant deception out of the propaganda pit of hell! That only just proves how incredibly gullible and undiscerning we really are in our battle for truth and freedom. The truth is, even though we all have sinned, sinning does not make us depraved any more than falling down makes us a bad, though the fall may have injured us and seems to have convinced many of us that we cannot walk.

If I see myself as innately unholy and bad and if that is my first (original) nature, then, sadly enough, I must conclude that I carry no glimmer of God or His nature within me. His image is completely absent from my life, and I live a pointless, tormented life torn between trying to please God and giving up!

If I believe everything I see, I will believe that what I see myself doing is who I am. As I see myself sinning, lying, stealing, fornicating, killing, I will conclude I am a liar, a thief and a pervert. If reality defines me to be what I see and feel and think and do, and if I hold reality to be the truth, and my reality tells me I am all the things I see myself doing, if I see myself sinning I must conclude I am sinful and bad. If I am bad, then I deserve to be condemned and punished because I am guilty. The depravity of man doctrine mocks the power of the Cross of Jesus Christ because if I am depraved, nothing could save us.

Therefore, according to human logic and reasoning, which also dominates the thinking of many who claim to be part of the body of Christ, if I sin, I am a sinner. If the Enemy can trick me into "doing" the things I hate, he can get me to "hate" myself. If I do the things "I hate", does not my very "hatred" for the things I do suggest a moral repulsion of those things in my conscience. How can I have a conscience, if I am depraved?

And if the things I see myself doing are so natural, and innate as to who I am, why would I fight 'bad behavior'? Why wouldn't I hail it as wonderful and right? Why do I feel guilty when I sin if sinning is part of my true nature? After all, dogs do not feel guilty for barking nor do they apologize for barking when they wake you up, because barking is part of being a dog.

Guilt can only work if it has something to work against. Why do I feel bad when I sin and violate my conscience if I were built to sin in the first place? Guilt is the first and most sure evidence that I am not in agreement with the sin I did, because if that thing was really 'me', there would be no conflict with it. I would feel no condemnation for doing it. If sin and sinning are the correct definition of who we are and truly a part of our original nature, why would we feel guilty for sinning at all? Why would we ever want to change or repent? And if we see no need to change or repent, why would we want to cooperate with the grace of God that invites "whosoever will" to come unto Him to be saved?

Why would we suffer so greatly from the shame and separation sin causes us if we didn't care about goodness or holiness or God, in the first place? There would be no struggle, conflict, guilt, suffering or regret over sin. There would be no war going on inside of me between good and evil if I were innately and inherently evil.

Any look-a-like truth we put in the place of TRUTH in our mind becomes a source of demonic deception and bondage. The devil can use both bad behavior and good behavior to advance his schemes against us. He uses bad behavior as a lever to stretch our divine nature on his torture rack as he works to redefine us in the light of his definition of us and our sinful human nature. This causes us to believe we are bad because we do bad things or, as many children conclude, 'I must be bad because bad things happen to me', and 'I am bad because I feel bad.'

Satan can also use good behavior and our desire to 'be good' which comes out of our divine nature, to provoke us to use religious means to obtain righteousness. This sets in motion a vicious cycle of performance and failure that leads to trying harder, which ultimately wears us out and un-motivates us in the pursuit of the things of God.

BASED ON FEELINGS

If the Enemy can shift the definition of our identity onto a 'feelings' platform, it will no longer be based on the Word of God. He can then manipulate our feelings by manipulating the circumstances upon which those feelings are based. If our identity is based on feelings and external happenings instead of internal security, all Satan has to do to 'take us out' is mess up our environment and get us to feel bad or guilty for it being our fault.

The Word of God admonishes us to walk in the Spirit. That means we do not walk or make decisions according to our feelings or our thinking. We are told to walk by faith, not by sight. If I form my conclusions and rest my identity on my feelings and what I see myself doing, the devil can convince me I must change my bad behavior to be good. In order to change my bad behavior, I must change my feelings. Trying to manage my feelings to get victory over bad behavior is an exercise based on futility and is impossible.

Even in the natural, facts are not based on feelings. My identity as my earthly father's daughter does not change just because I don't feel like I am his daughter today. Feelings do not change the facts? Even though sinning makes us feel bad and misleads us concerning the health and vitality of our relationship with God, if I know that I do not want to sin, nor was I created to sin, I can know that what is going on in me is not me, but the sin that dwells in me. (Rom. 7:20)

If I am listening to the Liar's counsel, and not the Lord's, sin presses me to take responsibility and repent. True repentance, however, comes when we stop believing the lie(s) and come into agreement with the truth as God has given it to us through His Word. Jesus said to "Repent and believe in the Gospel." (Mk. 1:15) The true Gospel tells me who I am and what God has said about getting into heaven.

When we sin, we are instructed to confess our sin and come back into agreement with the truth. Repentance and confession restore our relationship with God. When we submit to God we have strength to resist the devil and all his temptations and suggestions to fix our problem ourselves. Using the Enemy's solutions to resolve the issues of guilt and sin only drive us deeper into the pit of shame and condemnation.

There is no merit to self-improvement or doing it ourselves when it comes to sanctification and overcoming sin. We only prevail against our Enemy through the provisions of forgiveness and righteousness that come through our relationship with Jesus Christ. Jesus Christ "whom God set forth to be the 'propitiation' for our sin" (I Jn. 2:2) allowed God to 'pass over our sins' because the Blood of the Lamb had already taken care of the debt of sin.

IT'S NOT TO BE ALL ABOUT ME

When my focus is on my sin or my feelings, my life is suddenly, all about me instead of all about Him. If I am a 'sinner' because I sin, (do sins), I must take responsibility for my actions and do something to stop sinning. I can either cry out, "O, wretched man that I am," and ask, with Paul, "Who will deliver me from this body of death?" (Rom. 7:24) or I can embrace the suggestions of religion as my guide in spiritual matters and try to be good.

The Bible's solution to sin and the problems it creates is not to get my to 'take responsibility' or 'try harder to be good', but to DIE. Romans 6:11 releases us from the hold of the law of sin and death through death. Paul tells us to reckon the "old man" dead and reminds us in Galatians 2:19 that we have been crucified with Christ.

When Adam and Eve sinned they embraced the shame of having sinned, done something bad, and immediately took up the responsibility of fixing it by covering their nakedness (shame) with fig leaves. They also hid. Shame drove them away from God. Sin separated them from goodness, both their own and God's. They became afraid to be in the presence of God so they fled into darkness to cover what they could not bear to look at themselves.

Therein lies the fatal flaw in embracing my actions as the definition of who I am, and excusing them by claiming I'm only human. I am not "only human". I am a far cry from anything the devil has to say about, 'Who I am'. I know he uses the 'reality' of my 'sin' to persuade me to embrace the responsibility and religious duties he gives me to 'fix' that sin and get rid of it. If I did not hate sin in the first place, nothing Satan would have to offer me as a remedy for sin would be of any interest to me.

Fig leaves never worked in the garden. They do not work in the church. Man's attempts to clean up his own sin only make things worse, especially when considering the waste of precious time and life we spend on the futility of personal redemption. Justifying our religious activities as being a true expression of holiness and elevating them to the level of true spiritual worship, when they are not, is another cunning twist of Satan's plot against us.

AM I A SAINT OR A SINNER?

How we see ourselves then, becomes critical to winning the battle over sin. How do you see yourself? As a sinner? As a saint? The bible calls us 'saints'. As a sinner saved by grace that still sins? What? Who am I and who will tell me the truth? Am I good or am I bad or both?

Our natural inclination is to believe what we see and perceive ourselves to BE is defined by the thing we see ourselves DOING. Seeing myself doing bad things is a simple argument Satan makes to convince me, 'I am bad!' If I believe 'I am bad', what hope do I have except to try very hard to do better, or to give up? I am stretched on the torture rack that Paul described in Romans 7, doing the things I don't want to do, and not doing the things I want do.

If our self-concept is formed by our perceptions of ourselves, based on what we see ourselves doing, our behavior becomes the basis of our identity. When 'doing' defines 'being', we confuse 'doing bad things' with 'being bad'.

God defines us as Human BEINGS. Satan would define us as human DOINGS because when he gets us to DO something wrong, (which is very easy for him to do), he can come back at us with the argument, 'Look what you did! Who do you think you are?' 'It's your fault, you are guilty.' Satan uses the simple argument, 'You did it' to convince us that we are BAD. When we see ourselves doing bad things we have no case to stand on to resist the devil's argument; 'YOU did it (the sin) therefore, YOU are BAD'.

Though the question of sin may seem to address behavior more than identity, we form our self-concept largely by what we do, and how we feel about what we do, regardless of the truth of what the Word says about who we are in Christ. One of the most subtle and critical places for us to believe the truth of the Word is in this matter of identity.

We take the first step to freedom when we agree with what God says about who we are, regardless of how we FEEL about ourselves. When talking about defining our identity, the Apostle Paul admonished us, saying, "I do not even judge myself." (I Cor. 4:3) Judging ourselves is a temptation most of us fall headlong into and never recover from.

MY RELATIONSHIP WITH SIN   79

DEPRAVED OR DECEIVED

'I am bad' is not the same as 'I do bad things'. The Bible does not call us bad but is full of stories of people who did bad things, and what happened to them as a result. Many people get an incorrect idea of what all that means and assume people sin because they are bad, which appears to be a reasonable conclusion. That conclusion, however, does not match up with other things that God tells us about sin

In I John 1:8-10, we are told that "If we say that we have no sin, we deceive ourselves, and the truth is not in us. If we confess our sins, He is faithful and just to forgive us our sins and to cleanse us from all unrighteousness. If we say that we have not sinned, we make Him a liar, and His word is not in us."

This passage is written to BELIEVERS. It is very clear that even after we are saved, we will sin. In the same book, I John 3:5-10, however, John says, "Whoever has been born of God does not sin, for His seed remains in him; and he cannot sin because he has been born of God." So, unless we change our logical and limited interpretation of sin and how it affects the sons of God, God's Word does not make sense and we are confused. Confusion is not of God.

Often times things appear to be contrary or different from one another even though they are describing the same thing. The only explanation for the conflicting conclusions in examining the exact same thing, in this case, 'sin', is that the issue is being described from two different perspectives. From God's point of view - perspective - "Whoever has been born of God does not sin, His seed remains in him and he cannot sin." (I Jn. 3:9) But from our perspective, the verse right before that says, "He who sins is of the devil." (I Jn. 3:8)

So as we can see, from God's perspective, our sins are covered by the Blood of Jesus and we are seen as righteous. From our limited finite view, we are still trying not to sin, but failing. God sums up the matter by saying, in I Jn. 3:20, "For if our heart condemns us, God is greater than our heart, and knows all things." God gets the final word on how we are judged, even if we judge ourselves as condemned.

The scripture is clear. God did not make us bad. He made us in His Own image, precious and pure. Even after Adam and Eve sinned, God reiterated the enduring truth of man being made in His image, even after the Fall and the Flood when He told Noah in Genesis 9:6 "whoever sheds man's blood, by man his blood shall be shed; For in the image of God He made man."

WHERE DID EVIL COME FROM

For the Bible to be a valid resource manual for the explanation of life it must be able to explain the existence and propagation of both good and evil in the world and man as created in the image of God. In addition, any formula we would use to reduce all the diverse elements of experience to their proper origin must include the freedom of choice, a neutral creation and a wicked disregard for God that tampers with God and His relationship with His creation.

The equation used to explain 'all the evil we experience in the world', must include not only God and us, but also Satan. One of the Enemy's most blatant deceptions is to convince the world and Christians specifically, that the devil does not exist. He is nearly forgotten, except in the movies, or as some ancient medieval character that has vanished like a vapor since the dawn of our advanced technology. If the devil is not put in the equation used to explain 'life on the planet', and 'God plus us' must account for all the trouble we see in the world, then either God must be bad or we must be bad, i.e., responsible for all the evil present in the world.

Nothing can clearly be understood as long as a question of its true origin remains. If the origin of a thing can be established, so can its nature, power, effects and intentions. We must also understand that the Bible only describes two (2) kingdoms, not three (3). Those two kingdoms are Heaven and Hell. There is no kingdom of ME. I do not have a kingdom, nor does MY FLESH have a kingdom though I may seek to control the world around me.

Regardless of my desire for power, I will end up in one of the other two kingdoms for all eternity when this earthly life is over. Therefore, the kingdom of my flesh or 'me' cannot be used in the final definition or explanation of things or destinations. We will, however, have to give an account of our decisions and understand that 'free will' becomes the pivotal point and perfect opportunity for Satan to pin on us all the stuff he gets us to choose to do in the exercising of our free will.

The Tempter is like the slick salesman who has studied his potential clients, their demographics, and the psychology of sell-ing, to persuade his targeted population to buy his snake oil remedies for their human ailments. Since the Wicked One has set up every manner of human ailments, his customer base is guaranteed. Eager to find his quick fix, short-cut methods to peace and the 'good life', they are very interested in what he has to offer them and easily persuaded. Little do they know that his snake oil solutions are inflated with hidden costs and full of poison.

He then justifies himself and his sly devious intentions to harm us by reminding us we bought it, we agreed to it, we used it, and he is no longer responsible for what happens to us because we agreed to use it. And yes, maybe no one was there to physically force us to do it, but rarely is anyone there to warn us of its dangerous nature, either. We were easily taken advantage of and caught on the hook of his smooth sales pitch and deliberate deception.

And even though we are not depraved, it is clear, we can easily be deceived. Combining our ignorance and naiveté with the devil's intense and deliberate intention to deceive us; and given our free will to choose or refuse the truth, the possibility for sin and transgression are endless. Satan complicates God's simple solution to the pervasive problem of sin and blames it on us.

IT'S HIS FAULT

If Satan can conceal his existence or deceive us into taking the blame for the evil he does, he can build his case against us, both inside our own minds and in the Court of Heaven. He must prove that we are bad and get us to agree with it. Our agreement with guilt allows him to legitimize his case for religious legalism and his actions against us as a defense of the law. He comes looking like one who lifts up the law all the while he is tempting us and then condemns us for breaking it.

Approaching the destruction of creation from the angle of trying to regain what we lost in Eden and take control of our circumstances allows the Enemy to capitalize upon our innate hatred of sin and our desire to be good. It increases his leverage and opportunity to torment us on the torture rack of 'try harder, and never enough'. We fail and feel unworthy of God's love. Religion pushes the blame on us and the Enemy convinces us that he is right, and we deserve to be punished. All forms of demonic punishment include pain.

Satan uses deception and the lie to separate us from God. He uses our own efforts to stop sinning to trick us into sinning. He knows a kingdom divided cannot stand. Through the lie, Satan sets us up in opposition to ourselves, as we come to see ourselves as our own worst enemy. What tragedy awaits us as we attempt to defend ourselves in <u>that</u> battle?

DEPRAVITY GLORIFIES RELIGION

Depravity opens the door to a world that glorifies works and religion as the means of salvation and not the Christ of God. It twists the meaning of grace and makes salvation a thing to be earned. It makes God out to be cruel, selective, partial and prejudiced. A savior of the select-elect nullifies 'grace' and makes salvation a matter or good works. Religion makes me a 'transgressor' and cancels out the work of the Cross, making the sacrifice of the Son of God pointless. (Gal. 2:16-21)

If man is depraved, then the whole plan of salvation as given through the Gospel and written in the scriptures and deposited in our hearts by the Holy Spirit is wrong. The doctrine of the depravity of man is a deception that destroys man and glorifies Satan. For us to walk in truth, we must embrace a simple, uncomplicated, explanation of the presence of evil in the world that allows us to both explain the presence of evil and the power of the Gospel. If even one of those explanations are wrong, we are deceived.

The Bible says that when we were "without strength" (Rom. 5:6) and "dead in trespasses," God "made us alive together with Christ (by grace you have been saved)" (Eph. 2:5). Being dead to sin in not the same as being deceived or depraved. The doctrine of depravity undermines grace and the freedom of election that comes through the Cross itself. If there is no scriptural support for the idea of the depravity of man, it is, at best, a theological assumption and at worst, a demonic wormhole that has eaten into the fabric of our relationship with God.

DID JESUS HAVE A DEMON

Jesus was both divine and human. IF human beings brought forth after Adam and Eve had somehow become depraved, Jesus

Himself, born of a woman, would also have been depraved. If He had even one atom of depravity in His nature, He would not have been qualified to go to the Cross as a pure, spotless offering for sin.

Satan incited a riot against Jesus from the moment He was born, until He hung on the Cross. He persuaded the Jews who accused Jesus of "having a demon" (Jn. 8:48) when, in fact, it was Jesus who had come to expose the devil and his demons who had worked behind the scenes, fairly unhindered since the beginning of time. No one had been able to effectively challenge them or knew how to protect themselves or their family from them.

When Jesus came on the scene He was like a paramedic with the power to heal without the application of emergency equipment. He came with an authority the demons recognized and submitted to. He handled them with dutiful respect and when He went to the Cross He declared that He would prevail against His Enemy because, "the ruler of this world ... has nothing in Me." (Jn. 14:30) Jesus was clean. The devil had nothing on Him. Everything Satan was about to do was completely illegal and unjustified. He would pay dearly for the crimes he was about to commit against the LORD, by being literally and eternally cast into the Lake of Fire at the judgment.

The truth Jesus brought from heaven was unrecognizable to those who were of this world, whose eyes were closed and whose ears were shut. They were not able to "understand his speech", or "listen to His words". They had been born blind and deaf, hardened and unresponsive to the truth that Jesus brought, because they were "of this world". They could not understand the language of the Kingdom of God because they were "not of God". (Jn. 8:44 &47) "You are of your father the devil," He said. They were of the nature and disposition of the devil, not the offspring of the Lord God.

The Greek word for 'father', (Pater) used in this passage means, "one who resembles another in disposition and actions, as children usually do their parents." See Pg 929, item #3962 in The Complete Word Study New Testament, by Spiros Zodhiates, TH.D. The Greek word (Patria), which comes from the word Pater, is used to denote "What belongs to or springs from the father, his family, descendants". The Father (Pater), is represented as having only one (Patria), family. This indicates the oneness of God's family, both Jews and Gentiles, both those saints of the OT as well as of the NT, who were all baptized into the body of Christ, see Acts 2, 10, 11, 19 and I Cor. 12:13).

Jesus exposed the nature and disposition of those who believed and promoted lies as an indictment against the Jews and all others who do not believe what He taught as true. Deception was keeping them in darkness. They could receive neither the truth or walk in the light because Isaiah's tragic observation was true, "(this people) keep on hearing, but do not understand; keep on seeing, but do not perceive." (Is. 6:9) What a sad comment upon the state of man. How it must grieve the Father Heart of God to see us so estranged from Him and entangled with His enemy.

Notice, at no place does Jesus call his accusers demons, even though He minces no words in identifying them as "hypocrites and whitewashed tombs" (Mt. 23:23 & 27) and "of their father the devil." (Jn. 8:44) Rather, He talks about truth and their not being able to receive it. (Jn. 8:45-47) Even in their rebuttal, the Jews did not say Jesus was a demon, though they strongly implied Jesus "had a demon."

They understood that demons and humans were two separate classes. This however, did not exclude the idea that a human could, 'have' or host, a demon, though, 'having a demon' might more correctly be identified as being 'controlled and occupied by a demon', as opposed to being 'owned' by it. They under-stood the concept of 'demonization' as one who is being deceived by a demon and that those who were, were demonized.

Even the man filled with demons, (Mk. 5:5-6) also known as the Demoniac, was able to fall down in front of Jesus and worship Him. If he would have been totally depraved, which defines man's origin as inherently wicked, he would have had no interest in God or any desire to repent or acknowledge his sin. He would never have come to Jesus or received ministry from Him in the first place.

Deception leads to being controlled by demons. Being controlled to varying degrees is called demonization. Demonization means being filled with and controlled by the lies of the Liar. When we are consumed with bitterness, guilt, anger, condemnation, which twists into self-bitterness, and self-condemnation, we give up on ourselves and the light of God's truth inside us begins to dim

We begin to yield to hopelessness and despair, even to the point of hating ourselves, others, and God. We give up on being good enough to be saved and cast off all restraint. We lose the vision for our lives. We give ourselves over to believing we are never going to make God happy and go away from the love and promises of God. We slip into a place of dismay and powerlessness, which is right where sin and Satan want us.

CAN A CHRISTIAN HAVE A DEMON

If 'responsibility' is not a biblical word, we do not find it in the Bible - we must conclude the word 'responsibility' is a human word created by the Enemy as a 'hook' on which to catch us. He is using vocabulary and semantics to get us to take responsibility for what the Enemy is doing in and through us. (I know most Christians deny the presence of demons acting out or living inside of, or controlling a 'saved, born-again' believer, but that is not what the Word of God says).

We are deceived into drawing conclusions based on some very faulty and erroneous assumptions. There is not one scripture in the Word of God that bear witness to the assumption that a Christian cannot have a demon. There is no scripture that says a 'Christian' cannot be 'controlled' or 'inhabited' by an evil spirit, although we cannot be 'owned' by both God and Satan at the same time. To the contrary, we see even the Apostle Paul call our attention to this invasion of our house. (II Tim. 2:24-26) Jesus also warned us in Matthew 12:29 and Luke 11:21 about the one who comes as the 'stronger man' to divide the house, take away our weapons and plunder our goods.

To be clear, Salvation settles the question of ownership in the believer's life. Sanctification, on the other hand, is an ongoing process, much like life begins the process of living. So too, sanctification is the process of cleansing the house and deprogramming us from the 'body of death' Paul talks about in Romans (7:24). What Paul describes as a body of death could just as easily be described as a corrupt software program running in the soul.

ANGEL OF LIGHT

The Gospel of John starts out with "In the beginning was the Word, and the Word was with God, and the Word was God. ...In Him was life and the life was the light of men. ...that was the true Light which gives light to EVERY man who comes into the world....But as many as received Him, to them He gave the right to become children of God, to those who believe in His name;..." (Jn 1:1, 4, 9, & 12)

Jesus calls Himself the Light of the world, but He also warns us about the "angel of light" who comes looking like Him, and bringing with him those who look like ministers of righteousness when, indeed, they are ministers of death. (II Cor. 11:13-15) God gives light and faith to everyone who comes into the world. That gives us the ability to recognize Him and the light that bears witness to the Truth.

Through the light of that revelation, everyone is given the right to become a child of God. "Whosoever will" can call upon the name of the Lord and be saved. (Rom. 10:13) Does this sound like the gospel of selective salvation or selective election where some are saved by grace and others are not? "God is not willing that any should perish, but that all should come to repentance." (II Pet. 3:9) God , however, will not force anyone to follow or serve Him or go to Heaven. The Word of God says, "whosoever will call upon the name of the Lord will be saved". (Rom. 10:13) God does not lie!

Jesus warns us to beware that if the light that is in you is in darkness, how great is that darkness. (Mt. 6:22) That means, if the thing I believe to be true is given the place of truth in my life, but is not truth, it will bring me into bondage and deep deception. Satan himself transforms himself into an "angel of light" (II Cor. 11:14). He brings a false light that reflects a counterfeit truth and ultimately, a counterfeit gospel. If we embrace the counterfeit or any part of it as true, it will bring us into deception.

God and Satan are at war with each other and we are caught in the crossfire between the Truth and the lie that is made to look like the truth. That war reduces down to one between the truth and the lie. In this battle the Enemy tries to set us up in "opposition to ourselves." He sets our spirit up against our soul to challenge our faith. Confusion sets up a debate between Faith, (our spirit) and Reality, (our soul). Is the truth defined by what we experience and have come to believe as real and therefore, believe to be true, or is truth defined by what God says in His Word?

The winner is determined by whose report we choose to believe. Victory over the darkness is settled when we can discern the difference between who is telling us the truth and who is lying. Fortunately God has sent the Holy Spirit whose job it is to lead us into "all truth". Without Him, we have no hope of trying to discern or protect ourselves from the treachery of the lie.

TO CONSIDER AND EXAMINE

Evidence of the "angel of light" masquerading as truth in your life can be seen in the level of rest and freedom you are experiencing in your spirit. You may be in trials but they are not to be confused with 'bondage'. If the trials have not kept you from loving unconditionally, rejoicing in persecution, or forgiving as often as necessary, they are opportunities for growth and refinement, not bondage. Bondage brings condemnation and confusion.

Bondage can look like many things. Too often we become so familiar with our 'lot in life' that we do not recognize it as anything unusual. We accept our experiences as divinely ordained and take a soft, passive, almost fatalistic approach to our lives and what goes on in them. Life is just too precious to take for granted and be lived at such a shallow level. God invites us to climb over to His side and see what He has for us. Some of us are trying 'too hard' to make something out of our lives, while others are giving up too quickly in their determination to 'fight the good fight of faith' and break out of the ruts.

Do you know the 'rest' of abiding or are you exhausted trying to rest? Are you feeling irritated, fearful, anxious, or chronically ill? Are you experiencing on going setbacks and difficulties in your life?

LIES = BONDAGE | BONDAGE = LIES

- Look for specific bondages in your life. Now the question becomes, not what are the bondages, but what are the lies that hinder me and set up those bondages? Ask the Lord to show you the lies you are believing that the Enemy is using to create those setbacks.
- TRUTH sets us free, not Good Works. Truth says, "Whom

the Son sets free is free indeed." (Jn. 8:36) What is the truth
He wants you to know?

- Have you changed your mind on how you thought about
sin or how you felt about committing it?

* * *

CHAPTER 5

MY RELATIONSHIP WITH OTHERS

My relationships with others begin with a few basic ones in a limited geographic area, and can expand to include an indefinite number of friends, family and acquaintances spread around the world. Though we usually only have a few close and significant relationships, the number of possible meaningful relationships grows as we join clubs and organizations and embrace creeds and participate in ideologies.

Relationship categories can generally be broken down several ways. They are either by blood or by agreement. They may be entered into willingly or reluctantly. They may begin with hope and promise and end tragically or they may begin poorly and end nicely. They are unpredictable, volatile, dynamic, and like any living thing, need to be watered and nurtured to do well.

The first and basic role everyone must accept in the drama of human life is that of a child. Every role or position we hold requires and is defined by relationship. As a child, we all have a mother and a father, though they may leave after the first few moments of conception or after the first few hours of birth. And though we may never see them again, or sit in their presence, their genetic coding and generational legacy will be revealed in us as specific patterns that define our appearance and preferences, including the way we do relationships.

IT'S NOT FAIR

Some of us come into this world wanted and celebrated; others come unwanted and endangered. No one gets to pick his or her parents, their socio-economic status, their time in history, or nationality. That is why it is foolish to credit yourself for deserving a grand life because you were born into a station of good fortune or conversely, to see yourself as 'less than' because you were born into a place of poverty and want. We all start out as God permits, and definitely, not on equal footing.

To pride ourselves on having worth, based on nothing we did or based on our own strength is presumptuous and pathetic. To think we are 'better than' someone else based on looks or brains or a divine endowment of talent is a set up for arrogance, self-righteousness and tragedy. What will we be when our beauty fades and our body grows old and we cannot perform any longer? What 'good thing' is someone 'entitled to' that all do not deserve

All of these differences and discrepancies place us in the middle of injustice and unfairness. Injustice and the bitterness it breeds can become the theme song of life and the undoing of relationships. Anger and sensitivity to injustice provokes even the most peace loving among us to rise up and resist. We get tangled up in circumstances and begin to shape our ideas of life, relationships, and reality out of whatever raw materials have been handed to us. If what we are given is not the truth, it is junk! Whenever we build with that which is not truth we are brought into bondage.

TRUE WORTH

The basis for true worth comes from the One Who made us and what He was willing to pay to get us back. Many of us, however,

show little regard for God or what He thinks, or how much He gave to pay off our kidnappers from Hell. We are too busy trying to figure out what everyone else thinks about us and judge ourselves worthy by what they say about us rather than consider His sacrifice or its implications on our worth or the worth of others.

Unfortunately other people's opinions about my worth are not based on my true market value as established by God, but are set by the social standards of worldliness, convenience and selfishness. If I am an inconvenience, a bother, in the way, born the wrong sex, or do not match the expectation of those who will be my first caretakers, I will be shaped by their disappointments and spend the rest of my life trying to cancel out their rejection.

The words and actions of others are initially more powerful in influencing me in how I see myself than any Word whispered over me by God. Though parents are only people themselves and carry many scares and wounds from their own childhoods, their power to influence my life and shape my destiny is frightening

Many parents never recover from their own childhoods in time to raise their children. As a result, many children suffer from 'father wounds' that continue to be passed down from generation to generation. The same wounds they suffered provide an open door for the rejection and failure they experienced to be passed down to the lives of their children.

JUSTICE FOR ALL

Little of lasting value can be done to stave off or correct the effects of negative parenting through natural means because the damage done was first spiritual and then physical. Education and all kinds of programs for the disadvantaged have been created at every stage of governmental intervention to help the displaced and the unloved. But even though these programs help some, there is no substitute for love in the 'equality equation'. Nothing can level the playing field for the poor, neglected and abused outside of the revelation of God's love for them.

With all of us starting out in different places, with different parents and different situations, we look for the common denominators that create common ground upon which equality and justice can stand. Only the Cross can take away the shame of sin and restore the glory stolen from us to make us all feel welcome and worthy. Life is more than full of enough opportunities for each of us to love and be loved. God has provided victory to prevail against the original odds we faced coming into the world as children when we started out at the mercy of others.

RATING YOUR RELATIONSHIPS

Even as the number of relationships we have may be small to begin with, the world is full of limitless possibilities. And though they all start out simple, they can very quickly become impossibly complicated. We find ourselves spending the bulk of our lifetime trying to untangle the mess and fix our relationships thinking if we can find out what went wrong, we can make it better.

We take on the job of fixing something we did not break. We try to solve the problems of fixing other people's happiness by controlling or blaming ourselves or others. We try to be perfect to get our parents to parent us. God and obedience to Him, however are the only solution to whatever ails us.

The list of relationships we are in can include, but are not limited to, God, myself, family, others, my life circumstances, money, food, trials, the government, etc. Feel free to add to the list yourself.

Now rate your satisfaction level in your relationships based on how you 'feel'. Though the just "shall live by faith" not 'feelings', 'feeling the feelings' helps us find the lies, because any part of our belief system not based on God is vulnerable to the Enemy defining us by how we 'feel'.

Next reevaluate your beliefs based on what the Word of God says is true. Here are your category ratings. I am loved (L), I am okay, (OK), I am not okay, (NOT), it needs work, (NW), I'm at a loss for words, (LW), it's my biggest stressor (S), it's too late, (TL), all things are POSSIBLE with (GOD)

- My relationship with God. (I Pet. 1:3)
- My relationship with myself. (I Cor. 15:10)
- My relationship with my others. (I Pet. 3:1, I Pet. 1:22)
- My relationship with my life circumstances. (Acts 20:24)
- My relationship with the Evil One. (Pr. 8:13, Pr. 16:6)
- My relationship with an enemy. (Pr. 24:17, Mt. 6:43-48)
- My relationship with affliction. (I Pet. 4:12)
- My relationship with my mate. (I Pet. 1-4 & Eph. 5:22-29)
- My relationship with my child. (Eph. 6:1-4)
- My relationship with my boss/as a boss. (Pet 2:18-22), (Eph.6:5-9)
- My relationship with a stranger. (Mt. 7:12)
- My relationship with the government. (Rom. 13:1-4, I Pet. 2:13-17)
- My relationship with suffering. (I Pet.3:8)
- My relationship with the world. (Jn. 15:18)
- My relationship with money. (Ja. 5:1-5)
- My relationship with sin. (Acts 13:38-39)
- My relationship with my job. (Pet. 2:18)
- My relationship with food. (I Cor. 6:12-13)
- My relationship with things. (Lu.12:15-21)
- My relationship with my church. (II Tim.2:24-26)

Score key: (L =5), (OK = 4), (NW = 3), (LW = 2), (S = 1), (NOT = 0), (TL = -1), (GOD = add enough points to = 100)

Add up your score. 100 – 80 Give God praise, life is great. 79 – 40 Rest in God and quit trying. 39 – 0 Jump for joy for the battle is the Lord's. 0 – -20 Rejoice, all things are possible with God.

WORDS AND DEEDS

Words form one of the major means of exchange in relationships. Words and deeds become the bricks and mortar of our relationships. Through experiences we learn how to lay those bricks in lines and rows. Relationships are a principle means of instruction in both teaching and learning about what life is and how life is to be lived. Rules, manners, and social skills must all be taught to ensure harmony and good will among men.

If our childhoods reflect the chaos and the dysfunction of our parents and care takers, we will know nothing more than they did and will end up suffering the same things they did. Godly instruction in truth becomes imperative to our survival and the continuation of civilization. The opportunities for Satan to interfere with and pervert our lives and those we learn from are endless. Much of what he does is twist our words both in our mouths and in the minds of the hearer to bring discord and chaos because he knows the power of words.

He knows that words form contracts and create concepts and become the working pallet of the mind to understand, and the will to do, and the heart to enjoy. Even as "death and life are in the power of the tongue," (Pr. 18:21) and "a good report makes the bones healthy," (Pr. 15:30) and "pleasant words are sweetness to the soul and health to the bones," (Pr.16:24) a bad report filled with critical, unpleasant, negative words, breaks the bones and crushes the soul.

Because words are living and powerful, they can build and bring us closer to the one who speaks them or they can tear us apart. We form our self-concept and settle the question of our lovability by examining the words of those around us. Their words become the well we drink from. If the well is poison, and we continue to drink from it, we will die

But, as destructive and mean and unkind as words can be, the absence of words can be even more deadly and disturbing. With no material to work with, we fill in the gaps with our own imagination and the subtle suggestions of the Evil One who is always available for comment. Without clear instruction, doubt and double-messages leave us baffled and uncertain. We cannot proceed with confidence in the tasks of childhood with such uncertainty.

Though most children may not feel safe or are informed enough to ask for help or even know what is wrong, the question of 'worth' forms the core of every child's being. 'Am I loved' is a question that must be answered before any of the other mysteries and challenges of life can be satisfactorily resolved. Silence leaves the person without understanding or direction. In the absence of information a vacuum is created that forces the child to take matters of concept formation into their own hands and figure things out for themselves. And we all know how disastrous that can be.

The tragedy of those first years is that we know nothing different from what we are told, nor do we apply critical thinking to our circumstances. Most of mankind does not have access to the truth of God's Word rightly divided. We have no solid frame of reference that can be applied to correct our thinking or bring us into a better relationship with ourselves or others. Our impressions are often mixed with fear and abandonment, which generate more isolation and alienation.

THE WORD INVENTORY

We often try to take an inventory of our worth and like-ability from those around us. We take too seriously the words they say while we deeply long to hear words they refuse to say. Only the Holy Spirit can grow us up to know who we are in Him, and accept ourselves for who He says we are. The tragedy of life is that most of us have never been correctly introduced to Him and so we feel alone and on our own.

- What were some key words and often repeated phrases you heard around your house growing up? (Caution: do not omit negative phrases, name-calling or swear words)
- What positive words did you hear or longed to hear that changed, or would have changed your life and how you saw it?
- Describe your sense of worth based on what you heard and how you interpreted those words.

SELF-ACCEPTANCE

St. Paul had one of the most tumultuous lives ever recorded. Rage and murder and pride and religious self-righteousness filled his early adulthood. After he got converted to Christ he was hated, chased, cast out, and arrested. Attempts were continually being made on his life. He was lied about, scoffed at and discredited.

His relationships registered every reading on the Richter scale from wrong to right, and yet, at the end of his heroic and life-threatening tour on earth, he could say, "by the grace of God, I am what I am" (I Cor. 15:10) and that "none of these things moved me". (I Cor. 15:10) What stability and sense of self did he possess that made him so sure?

He had become "settled and established" through his confidence in God. The externals of his surroundings lost their power over his mind and heart. Even sitting in jail seemed to be of minor consequence as he penned his last epistles to those on the outside. He knew that he belonged to Christ and that the life and power to live a supernatural life came from their relationship with each other through the Holy Spirit. Knowing who he was lifted the 'burden of proof' of his worth and value off of him and placed it where it was meant to be, on the Lord. Having peace with God made every-thing else all right.

LIBERATED

One of the most liberating of all self-concepts is to know that I am not my own, but that I have been bought with a price. Everything changes when we know, that "to live is Christ." (Phil.1:21) These are high concepts, and only attained through love and forgive-ness. Only those who are obedient and willing to surrender to the truth and choose to live for the glory of God and not man, can enter into that place of lasting peace.

Surrender of self is only fully possible when we know who we are. It was that knowing and surrender that made Jesus great. (Jn. 8:50-55) He was immune to the flattery and fleeting praise of fickle men because He was not dependent upon them for His value or affirmation. "He knew all men, and had no need that anyone should testify of man, for He knew what was in man". (Jn. 2:24-25)

Jesus said, "He who seeks to save (keep) his life will loose it and he who loses his life for My Sake will find (keep) it." (Mt. 25-26) This is the opposite of modern thinking where the survival of the fittest is praised and competition and self-exaltation are prized and applauded.

Most of us are not so inclined to live our lives with such abandon. To give up our life to save it seems absurd. The mind is at enmity with the idea of surrender and as long as we are carnal we will seek our solutions to life's problems through our own resources. Those of the world do not understand the things of God and cannot comprehend faith, or miracles, or mountains being removed by speaking to them. Minds were made to do math and mechanics and may be able to build a better mousetrap, but they cannot solve the deeper issues of morality or make men behave better or bring us peace.

TWO OPINIONS

It is bad enough for two different people to have two different opinions on the same subject, but when one person has two different opinions on the same subject, confusion rules. Many times, we are only in partial agreement with the decisions we make. We may waver between 'thinking' and 'feeling' for a long time. Confusion and 'I don't know' seem to be a place of middle ground that affords us a meager shelter and momentary comfort from the power of others who are ready to pronounce blame and demand their way.

Passivity and indecision rule as fear becomes our middle name, perverting justice and sound judgment. Feelings and thinking and "I'm not sure", cannot be the standards we use to measure the worth of another person or the relationship we will have with them. The inability to make sound decisions allows relationships to become abusive, unstable, and complicated. We waver as we work feverishly, to come to a decision to simplify our lives, trying desperately to arrive at a plan of action we can agree with.

Freedom comes in knowing truth. I can KNOW and then DO what is RIGHT in the sight of the ONE who does not change. He is not drawn into the fray to settle a personal offense, nor does He turn away in rejection, when He does not get His own way. He remains fair and impartial and acts out of truth and not impulse. This is the One we have full access to, to receive answers to difficult situations and people.

ISSUES IN OUR RELATIONSHIPS WITH OTHERS

Fear and love are opposite forces that both demand our attention. Fear sets up obstacles to love; love overcomes the obstacles of fear. When we listen to fear we are listening to lies and become victims. When we act out of love, we live in the truth and are victorious. Love sets us free to speak and be heard. Fear locks us up and makes us afraid to speak our own mind.

Fear and control often predominate in our relationships with others. Because survival as one of the core issues of life, fear promotes self by controlling others to insure optimum safety and the best results for our own personal welfare. Being alone and abandoned convinces us that we need to be in charge of what goes on, as no one else seems to have the time or be taking an interest in watching over me. I come to the foregone conclusion, 'it is up to me' and head down on life's pathway with 'me' as my guiding light.

Fear causes us to feel:

- Alone
- Abandoned
- Unprotected
- Needing to control our life
- Rejected
- Not safe
- Loved conditionally
- Not seen as good enough to be loved
- Seen as different

Love causes us to know we are:

- Loved unconditionally
- Supported
- Accepted

- Safe
- Seen as beautiful
- Seen as unique and loved for who I am
- Known and considered to be valuable

Unforgiveness causes us to judge injustices ourselves and hold the other person in judgment as a wrong doer until punishment can be administered. Unforgiveness causes us to:

- Stay angry, become bitter
- Hold grudges, preserve our rights
- Wait for the apology that never comes
- Make lists of offenses and crimes committed against us
- Hardens our heart and closes our eyes to any other way than our own

We are caught up in the 'principle' of wanting justice by staying mad and unforgiving. But, what is the cost of staying mad at someone? And is the price higher than we can afford to pay?

Conditional love sets expectations on love and bases love on performance causing us to:

- Strive for perfection
- Feel we need to justify our existence
- Reject ourselves based on another person's opinions of us
- Reject ourselves for our failure to provide for the wants and needs of others
- Feel unworthy of the love of another
- Look to another for affirmation and validation
- Feel less than, and not as good as
- Base worth on performance

Anxiety, depression, and stress exhaust us by making us:

- Strive to please others
- Try to do it right
- Feel like a failure
- Worry about what others say
- Try to manage what others feel, think and do
- Have to do it all myself
- Feel alone and it's all up to me
- Feel like I need to, I should, It is up to me

Indecisiveness destroys our clarity and confidence and makes us:

- Feel like I have no choice
- Have to make choices for others because they won't
- Believe I have no voice
- Afraid I will make the wrong choice
- Feel like it's up to me
- Feel like it's my fault
- Feel like I need to try harder, got to do more
- Feel like it's never enough
- Avoid making decisions

WORKING IT OUT

When our responses to others are contrary to what the Word of God says, our relationships break down and we live in bondage. Here are some of the things we do in our relationships.

We try to:

- People please (I Cor. 9:19-22)
- Become defensive (II Pet. 2:23-25)
- Judge ourselves (I Cor. 4:1-4)
- Trust others (Jn. 2:24-25)
- Judge others (Rom. 14:10-13)
- Get even (Ja. 1:20)

- Hold grudges (Eph. 4:26)
- Feel guilty (Acts 16:9)
- Build Walls (Is. 58:7)
- Fight and defend ourselves (Ja. 4:1)
- Curse our enemies (Ps. 37:7-8)
- Blame each other (Gen. 3:12)
- Worry and be anxious (Ps. 12:25)
- Fret (Ps. 37)
- Make things fair (Ps. 35:22-28)
- Avoid feeling like a failure (Ps. 66:8-12)
- I can't do it (Is. 41:10-13)
- I'm out of control (Lu. 21:36)
- I don't need anybody (Lu. 12:16)
- I'm offended (Mt. 18:7)
- I must 'Shut up!' (Lu. 21:15)
- I'm broke (Mt. 6:19-21)
- I'm better than you (Rom. 12:3)
- I'm afraid (Is. 41:10-13)
- I don't know what to do (Ps. 73:23-26)
- I'm worried (Mt. 6:34)

The Word says:

- Do I seek to please men or God? (Gal. 1:10)
- Jesus committed Himself to the Father (I Pet. 2:23)
- I do not judge my own self (I Cor. 4:3)
- Jesus did not commit Himself to man (Jn. 2:24-25)
- Let him without sin cast the first stone (Jn. 8:7)
- Repay no one evil for evil (Rom. 12:19)
- Pursue peace (Heb. 12:14-15)
- God will work it out in me (Phil. 2:13)
- Hiding from your own flesh (Is. 58:7)
- Feed your enemies (Mt. 5:44)
- Bless those who curse you (Mt. 5:44)

- Bear one another's burdens (Gal. 6:2)
- Be anxious for nothing (Phil. 4:6)
- Trust in God's Justice (Nam. 1:3)
- Lord is a righteous Judge (Nam. 1:7-8)
- I can do all things (Phil. 4:13)
- When I am weak (II Cor. 12:10)
- I know how to be abased (Phil. 4:12)
- I can of my own self do nothing (Jn. 5:19)
- Not to be offended (Lu. 7:23)
- Every idle word (Mt. 12:36-37)
- God shall supply (Phil. 4:19)
- The Lord has mercy on me (Lu. 19:11)
- Suffer wrongfully with patience (I Pet. 2:18-21)
- His Holy Spirit has been sent to lead us (Jn. 16:13)
- He is able to complete the work in me (II Cor. 9:8)

WHAT DO I DO WHEN

Match the problem with what you usually do in the situation. There may be more than one answer, but whatever the case might be, do not stress over your responses.

Problem:

- I am rejected by others
- I am ridiculed
- I feel unloved and unimportant
- I am misunderstood and misperceived
- I feel not listened to
- I am criticized
- I am given a double message
- I am betrayed by a friend
- I feel confused
- I don't trust my own feelings
- I get discouraged

- I feel slighted
- I am falsely accused
- I am lied to
- I am abused
- I give up
- I get jealous
- I get mad

Answer:

- I take it
- I keep quiet
- I pretend it didn't hurt
- I laugh it off
- I ask for more
- I smile and stay calm
- I know the truth
- I forgive
- I talk to a friend
- I get others to sympathize with me
- I take it out on someone else
- I give it back
- I bless those who persecute me
- I pray for those who spitefully use me
- I believe I am a victim
- I persevere
- I know I am secure
- I rejoice

In our human nature we are prone to become anxious, jockey for positions, feel isolated, feel mistreated, get offended, blame ourselves, mistreat others, act rudely and panic. Paul admonishes us to let go of the past and forget those things that are behind. We are called to press on (Phil. 3:13) and let God control our situations. (Phil 3:7-11)

The Bible is an invaluable resource guide to living which most people never use or look into for themselves. It has something to say about every human condition, teaching us how to live in and through difficult circumstances to bring glory to God. It teaches us to profit from those situations and gives us courage and grace to profit in all our tribulations.

FREEDOM FROM THE FEAR OF MAN

Paul said that he was not ashamed of the Gospel (Rom. 1:16). To be free and unashamed to do His will exclusively and regardless of what others think or say is freedom from idolatry and the fear of man. True freedom is demonstrated when our love for God causes us to live in obedience to Him and love His other children.

Obedience is the proof of our faith. To obey the Word of God in doing relationships becomes an act of faith in trusting Him to resolve the injustices in those relationships. He hears our crying. Faith says He will make it right and we will be restored because God is a just Judge and righteous in all His dealings with the sons of men.

Trusting God to judge fairly is the essence of forgiveness. Forgiveness is not becoming a doormat. It does not mean we cannot be angry. Nor do we, as Christians, have to deny that a crime was committed to prove we have forgiven.

Forgiveness acknowledges that a crime(s) has been committed and that we are submitting our case to the Court of Heaven to petition for the restoration of justice and mercy to us. Forgiveness says; we are not going to take matters of justice into our own hands. We surrender our case and the injustices committed against us to the righteous Judge of all the earth and wait for Him to vindicate us.

Forgiveness is based on trusting in the justice of God. Forgiveness will not happen if I do not trust God to bring forth justice. Anger and injustice will rule every relationship that is not lived out in a place of trusting in God to make things right. I can live free from anger and the fear of what man can do to me, because I know my Redeemer lives and He will vindicate me. I am free to love unconditionally and be who I am created to be because that is the only person I can honestly and genuinely be, anyway.

PLEASING GOD

Pleasing God simplifies life. Making Him happy is much easier than trying to please a thousand different people who are suffering from jealousy and have a million different ideas on what it will take to make them happy and how we should go about living our lives solely for their benefit.

And how can we compare ourselves with ourselves or to the expectations of others when comparisons are considered biblically unwise in the first place. (Rom. 11:25) Even more difficult and futile are those who would think it a worthy effort to try and meet performance's standards in its ever increasing demands for perfection.

If it is unsafe and impossible for me to determine who I am based upon what other people are saying about me, will I be wise to form a relationship with anyone based upon what they say about me? If their responds and projections and impressions of who I am are wrong or if I cannot be myself around them, but must pretend or comply with their demands, do I really have an honest relationship with them?

Do I have a real or healthy relationship, if I consider a bad, dishonest relationship better than no relationship at all? Am I willing to live in a relationship where I have to learn to live in the pain of rejection and stay there because I find it is less painful than having no relationships at all? Are these the relationships the Holy Spirit has commanded us to accept?

Paul called himself a servant of Christ and in serving Him, he had been set free from the opinions of men. He could become all things to all men (Gal. 1:10) and still not lose himself. He was OKAY. He had found he could be content in whatsoever state he found himself because he "knew in whom he had believed and was persuaded that He was able to KEEP that which he had committed to Him. (Phil. 4:11) Paul was unshaken in his confidence because his confidence was not in himself, or in his good deeds or in awards or the praise of men, but in God.

Paul was not a masochist. He was not trying to be a hero. He did not have a hidden agenda. He did not consider himself worthy or unworthy. He considered himself 'dead', crucified with Christ. Therefore, he did not consider what was required of him to be too much for God to ask. He could be an "offering poured out" and "rejoice in his sufferings for others." (Col. 24) He could count it, as did James, "all joy when we fell into various trials," most, if not all, of which have to do with relationships. (Ja. 1:2)

Paul was severely tested. His relationship with the Father was challenged from every angle through his relationships with those around him. Some loved him. Some abandoned him. Some did him much harm. The devil left no stone unturned in his examination of Paul's faith in regard to his relationships. But Paul had already passed the tests before they even began because he had chosen to submit all his tests to the Lord and let the Holy Spirit provide him with the best answers.

THE TESTING GROUND FOR LOVE

To walk in love is the mark of a true disciple; to bear one another's burdens fulfills the law of Christ. To love one another is the hardest and the greatest of God's commandments. Our Relationships with others becomes the crucible of suffering and the height of ecstasy that makes relationships the perfect testing ground for every human interaction. Love is God's standard for perfection and promotion.

Relationships provide the opportunities for love and faith to be proven. They provide opportunities, both great and small, for betterment or bitterness. They test, more than any other means, the faithfulness of God and the frailty of man. For the believer, relationships become the true test of character and obedience in making us into the man or woman God had in His mind when He made us.

No other condition or combination of circumstance known to man, have the power to create such adversity and challenge. We can walk on the moon and speak clearly to one another on the other side of the world but we often cannot walk softly or speak kindly to the one sitting across the table from us.

Every other relationship we have will ever have, and the quality of that relationship, is based on the relationship we have with ourselves. We are called to be a holy people (II Tim 1:9) and to "love one another fervently with a pure heart." (I Pet. 1:22) We are called to "lay aside all malice, guile, hypocrisy, envy, and all evil speaking." (I Pet. 2:1)

We are to "have our conduct honorable among the Gentiles, that when they speak against you as evildoers, they may, by your good works which they observe, glorify God in the day of visitation." (I Pet. 2:12) Peter instructs the younger disciples to honor others, love the brothers, fear God, honor the king and serve their masters well.

This is the same Peter who would have, in his younger days, gladly spear headed a movement against the resistance to Jesus, at the drop of a hat. His relationships with everyone changed dramatically after his conversion. He knew he was part of "a chosen generation, a royal priesthood, a holy nation, and part of His own special people". (I Pet. 2:9) It did not matter any more, that life was not fair or that he was judged as an "evildoer". What mattered was that God would be glorified, and in that, all was well with his soul.

LOVE

The most critical element necessary to the sustenance of human life is love. Love is essential to life, not optional. And though love is as indispensable to the human spirit as blood is to the natural body, many are forced to live without it by finding a substitute for it. Many live and die alone, never having known the love of God or of another human being. This is life's greatest tragedy!

The missing ingredient in most relationships is LOVE. The real definition of Love is 'to know and be known'. To love someone is to know that person and let them know you without being afraid they will reject you. Love lets us be vulnerable to another person at the deepest level of who we are.

If we are afraid to let others know us, if we hide ourselves, pretend to be someone else, cover up who we are, or hold back our true self because we do not feel safe, we will not know love or acceptance. Fear creates isolation and aloneness. "It is not good for man to be alone," God said in Genesis.

Love is the life-giving context in which any true relationships must be lived. When relationships are not lived within the context of love, they die. Love includes elements of safety, validation, confirmation, support, and availability. To be loved is to be wanted, prized, and cherished. Love promises to supply nurturing and works to remove lack. Love bestows honor and removes shame.

Relationships that are not based in love and truth cannot be true or good relationships. They cause us to lie and distort the truth about who we are. It is not safe to speak your mind or share your needs or ask for help. Love gives another person permission to speak their mind and make mistakes without retaliation.

Love does not judge by appearances and cares for the dignity of others. It treats all others, and especially those in close relationship, as sacred creations of God. Love corrects us with truth and trains us up in the Spirit to equip us for service. Love gives us a second chance and does not judge us as less than worthy, for taking it.

The Bible instructs us "not to love in word or in tongue, but in deed and in truth." (I Jn. 3:18) Giving lip service to the ideals of love is not love. Love is willing to go the any lengths to pay the price and stick around. "Love bears all things, believes all things, hopes all things, endures all things. Love never fails." (I Cor. 13:7-8) Love is not for cowards.

To love is not slavery or being enslaved to the desires of another. It is not defined as being used and abused, though at first glance they may look alike. We can only love with the intensity and sacrifice love calls for if we know who we are in Christ. Jesus Christ loved us with a perfect love. No one ever looks at the sacrifice He made for us and calls it abuse, though, in truth He was more hated and rejected and scoffed at and abused than any man that ever lived.

The reason we can go the second mile and turn the other cheek is because, 'it is NOT all about me'. It is about HIM and I KNOW who I am. Jesus knew who He was and that we were worth dying for. Of course, your love may be looked at by others as a foolish waste of time and unprofitable, or that the other person was 'not worth it.' The Bible tells us, there is a time for everything under heaven, a time to love and a time to leave. The question we need to ask then must be, 'What time is it?' That answer can only come from the Holy Spirit Who has been sent to lead us into all truth.

When all is said and done and all the excuses are made, Justice demands one thing; that we LOVE one another. The Bible simply says, "Owe no man anything but that you LOVE one another." (Rom. 13:8) Love is the debt we will never get done paying.

Justice is served when we serve one another with love because love serves another by doing for them and treating them the way you would like to be treated. We are priceless and precious and irreplaceable reflections of God's image, and carriers of His love, the essence of who He is.

What definition of love have you been using in your relationships with others?

CHAPTER 6
RELATIONSHIPS WITH DIFFICULT PEOPLE

W hat do we do when love fails? When we cannot bear the pain of the rejection or the misunderstandings or the twisted conversations or the paranoid projections being made against us anymore? When we cannot bear the injustices, the abuse, and the injury to ourselves or others we are responsible for? Who are we when our relationships get broken and our loved ones are driven away by treachery and the assaults of the Enemy?

Who are we then? When our world crashes down around us and we stand there, alone, rejected, misunderstood and slammed by the ones who used to open the door for us, the ones we held dear or hoped would love us in return? Are we going to take our identity from the painful words that rejection and bitterness and witchcraft hurl against us? Are we the same person we always were? Or will we ever be the same again? Have we become the 'pretend person' we thought they wanted us to be, to avoid what now can no longer can be avoided?

How do we overcome evil with good? How many times do we forgive before it is enough? Is Love more powerful than fear and hate? Does that mean I have to 'stay' in the relationship in order for love to prevail against the evil and destruction it brings into my life? Is my love for them courageous enough to forgive them and turn the injustices over to God and let Him help them face the fear in their own life?

And if it is, can I abide in peace, unafraid of losing them even when all appears to be lost? If I cannot trust the goodness of God to make things right, I will to continue to live in the grip of the fear of losing love, never realizing what I thought I had was never love in the first place. I had been living in the grip of fear all along?

DYSFUNCTIONAL RELATIONSHIPS

Fear offers many counterfeits for love. If the person we are in relationship with must control us in order to feel safe, and is not 'ok' with letting us be who we are, and we let them, neither one of us is 'OK'. Love says we are to bear one another's burdens, but not at the expense of losing our own identity. To give up my identity and divine calling to serve another is not serving God in truth, nor is it abiding in right relationship in serving one another. It is not 'losing myself' for the gospel's sake; it is idolatry.

If we surrender our will, including our desire to be true to our Creator, in order to make our earthly relationship 'work', we are caught in offering ourselves as a sacrifice to the insatiable appetite of the god of fear. These idolatrous, controlling, manipulative, narcissistic and intimidating relationships are not only very common but often end very badly. These types of relationships are defined by the secular world as 'abusive' and 'dysfunctional'.

The participants are seen as victims or abusers with the roles swinging back and forth between the two to make it very difficult to determine who is to blame. The spirits of blame and accusation use fear and control to create accusation and denial to perpetuate these deadly, abusive and dysfunctional relationships.

If difficult, unhealthy and demanding relationships describe the majority of relationships we are in, we need to take a look at the lies we believe that perpetuate those types of relationships. One of the most predominant of those lies is that we do not deserve anything better, or it is our fault things are going wrong. If most of our human energy goes into feeding an unhealthy relationship or trying to get out of one, we will be drained and discouraged. If we let other people's fears control us we are not free.

We must first recognize the true nature of the issue, including the lies we believe, before we can untangle ourselves from the enmeshment of the circumstances that surround that relationship. Many of these complications are entwined in a financial root of poverty that holds us captive to remain in a dangerous or difficult situation because we cannot afford to leave. Marriages held together by the glue of poverty and the fear of being homeless hold the members of that relationship hostage.

If the two people are married, the tearing apart of their 'one flesh' agreement in divorce, separates them again to a fate often more brutal than death. The energy of that bond is similar to the power released in the splitting of an atom with the damage being no less devastating. Worlds are torn up. Children are psychologically and spiritual broken. Lives are stunted and resource are poured into the wounded relationship to stop the hemorrhaging.

But who will dare to speak the truth. The truth heals, but the 'truth-teller' often becomes the first target to be mistaken for the enemy. "Do I become your enemy because I tell you the truth, Paul asked?" (Gal. 4:16) Even as our relationships become the testing ground for truth and the seedbed for love, do we love another enough to tell them the truth? Only the Lord God who is the defender of the defenseless can keep us from or deliver us out of the "grip" of the terrible one. (Is. 49:24-25)

Add to the conflict and confusion the twisting of the scripture that Satan can use on those who "refuse the love of the truth." (II

Thess. 2:10) God will permit the Enemy to send them, "a strong delusion that they should believe a lie." (II Thess. 2:10) In this we have the makings for a true disaster. Only God knows the hearts. Only God can judge our true intentions.

The good news is that even if our own hearts condemn us, God is greater than our heart and knows all things." (I Jn. 3:19-21) He can reverse the judgments we have come into agreement with under the counsel of the spirit of self-condemnation. Paul declared his wisdom in refraining from judging himself in I Corinthians 4:3 knowing the treachery of the Tempters to set him up in opposition to himself. (II Tim. 2:24-26)

The only right response we can make in these demonically engineered strongholds and snares that hold us captive is to cry out with the apostle Paul, "Who will deliver me from this body of death?" (Rom. 7:24) Only God can deliver us from this complicated mess of broken dreams and unattainable expectations that have broken our hearts. What can I do that I have not done, only leaves me to cry out like Paul, "Who" will deliver (rescue) me from this body of death?

CODEPENDENT CAR RIDE

Codependency can be defined as being married to, or in relationship with, someone who is being controlled by something or someone else. When we are relationship with someone who is being controlled by something else, we are vulnerable to also being controlled by the thing, (substance, illness, spirit) that is controlling them.

When we are in a codependent relationship with a person there is also a spiritual link to that person, be it a soul tie, business connection, contract or covenant. Satan can use those agreements and manipulate us through them. He is using them to gain control of and access to our life through our relationship with them.

Being in a codependent relationship with someone is like riding in a car with a drunk driver. You are sitting in the passenger seat speeding down the highway of life at recklessly high speeds. You become alarmed and begin to plead with the driver to slow down. You offer to drive for them or try to reach for the wheel yourself, all of which seems to have no affect on the driver as he/she flies down the road drinking and driving.

You panic. You yell. You threaten to jump out. You try to take matters into your own hands. All the while you keep glancing in the back seat at three terrified children buckled into their seats belts. You are trapped, afraid you may all soon be dead. You are determined to do something, whatever it takes to stop it. You cannot put yourself into that dangerous situation again.

The basic elements of any type of life controlling problem create a dangerous co-dependency for those in relationship with the Enemy's primary target, the main actor in the dysfunctional behavior. Remember, in all of these disrupting situations we are tempted to place blame and rehabilitate the person through human reasoning and religion, medical interventions and treatment programs. These remedies do not address the real issue or the root problems in the area causing the dysfunction nor can they stop the problem from being perpetuated.

How many of our lives end in tragedy because someone who lives his or her life in fear (insecurity) and rebellion controls ours? How many have dedicated themselves to "fixing" those kind of broken people because they 'feel sorry for them' only to come into a place of desperation and in need of help themselves?

TALKING TO THE DRIVER

After these kinds of terrifying experiences, most of us prefer to drive alone. Some continue to plead with the one on control. 'If you loved me, you would consider how your driving affects me', 'you say I just want to control you, but if you loved me you would change your driving habits out of concern for how it frightens me. You would be willing to change, out of your own freedom to love and care for me. If you loved me, my request would not be perceived as control. If you are perceiving my request as trying to control you, then you are not hearing me, or you are not listening to me with your spirit. You are being persuaded by an Enemy to take it personally'.

I CAN CHANGE HIM (HER)

The 'I can fix her/him fantasy,' has led to many a matrimonial car wreck. How many young men and women think their love for the other person is enough to make everything better, including anything they do not like about the other person. They dive into a dysfunctional relationship only to end up enabling their partner to continue on in his or her abusive behavior thinking they will stand by their man/woman, no matter what!

Real love is not being afraid to tell the truth and take a stand against fear and control. Real love is prepared to be misunderstood and does not reject when it is rejected. Many enter into marriage not understanding what price true love might cost them. Love prevails only after it has come of age through suffering and has died to itself in order to abiding in the will and love of God. Love is not afraid of what things look like or what the situation may call for. Love is not for cowards nor the faint-hearted.

If love is a feeling at all, the actual, hard-core feelings of love are more reflected in suffering than in elation. Love "bears all things, believes all things, hopes all things, endures all things" (I Cor. 13:7) and keeps on believing for God's will and His outcome in every bitter, unjust and painful situation. Love is both brave and wise. It knows how to suffer long and stay kind; how to love without envying and becoming jealous. It does not make more out of itself than it ought or become arrogant.

Love does not rejoice in bad things happening, even when the people who are doing the bad things to us may deserve it. It does not seek revenge and does not entertain evil and hateful scenarios in its heart. Love rejoices when others are blessed and when truth is exalted. Love knows when to stay and when to walk away. Love does not give up and go away though love may be asked to leave.

Love keeps on loving, even if it is only from a distance, that the soul of the offender may not be lost. This is the kind of love Jesus showed toward us, in that when we were still hostile and alienated from Him and the truth, He did not take it personally or get mad at us and give up on redeeming us from the grip of the one who had seduced us to believe his way was better than the Lord's.

BORN UNDER CONTRACT

Relationships do not just 'go bad' for no reason or over night. Neither is it all one person's fault. As innocent as we might think we are, and as high as our idealistic expectations might be for the relationship, the things that are controlling us now are also the things that have carried an assignment against us since our conception.

For this reason, many failed relationships go bad even before they begin. Before we are born, agreements have been made that continue to dictate our current state of affairs. We are not here to blame our ancestors, but the patterns of dysfunction have been set in motion through a long series of agreements with past generations that have been made without our knowledge. Our unawareness of them does not cancel them out or remove their demands.

These agreements set up the patterns of destruction that operate through the lies first believed by our ancestors. Our subconscious consent allows the Enemy to bring his demonic assaults, including the replication of past traumatic events still present in our bloodline, down upon us. He embeds himself in our temple, sets up strongholds, creates defense systems (run by protector demons), and conceals his activities through disassociation and denial. Disassociation is often used to cover the presence of the Evil one and his activities so we never even question what is going on or realize they are there. Abuse, unforgiveness, secret sins, crimes and injustices, iniquities, and unrequited acts of ill-will all facilitate the Enemy's work among us by opening the door for him to come in and "plunder the house". (Mt. 12:29)

Because of the unresolved injustices, fear becomes the bottom line the Enemy uses in the control and the breakup of any and all of our relationships, including the one we have with ourselves. Fear, insecurity, and offenses, the unresolved conflicts of childhood - past hurts that have not yet been resolved - and the need for control, all push love aside and open the door to a spiritual battle most of us are ill equipped to deal with.

When we add to our own personal conflicts, wounds and survival strategies to those of our mate, it is only a matter of time before the relationship begins to unravel, unless the spiritual issues are addressed through the truth of God's Word. Jesus said, "you shall know the truth and the truth will set you free". (Jn. 8:32) The testimony of His witness as to what really happened in our lives is the antidote to the bondage fear and the lie bring.

CAUGHT OFF GUARD (DEALING WITH OTHER PEOPLE'S DEMONS)

The DNA carries all the genetic codes and patterns that shape our genotype and the basic expression of those traits known as our phenotype. All the genetic information including those responsible for our overall health, aptitudes, dispositions and predispositions, (including our inclinations toward good and bad habits) are carried on the DNA.

The DNA also carries the marks of sin and iniquity as established by the generational agreements made by our ancestors. It provides the mechanism for the transfer of evil and demonic activities from one generation to the next. These marks of sin damage and alter the DNA. These areas, weakened through our generations agreements with sin, provide the familiar spirits the access they need to create emotional and physical patterns of distress and dysfunction in our lives. These patterns influence behavior.

These generational 'familiar spirits' hold permissions and operating privileges in the life of each new member of that bloodline. The child is being programmed, even in utero. Many people reject the idea of generational curses as unscriptural, however, there are many scriptures that speak to the existence of generational curses and the consequences of sin and iniquity being passed down into the lives of the children. If the Enemy has been given claim to any part of our body, soul, or destiny through those generational agreements, the evil fruit of those agreements will follow us and affect our relationships unless the sin is addressed and the agreements broken.

They penetrate and pervert (twist) our relationships, including our marriages, in making multiple and ongoing attempts to divide our house. When we marry, we do not realize that our spiritual 'baggage' is now added to the other person's to create a new, more complex and intense set of problems. Simply put, when we marry, we enter into an agreement with, and come under the influence and control of the other person's 'demons'. Though we are totally unaware of these 'third-person impersonators', they are real. They have come to trouble us and 'set us up in opposition,' not only to our own self, but to the one we married. They are hidden but they are there.

THE THIRD-PERSON IMPERSONATORS

The third-person impersonators are spirits that influence us by projecting a negative concept of the other person onto our mind and heart. This negative impression is promoted as the truth and becomes the new filtering system through which we begin to see the other person. We form our idea of who they are by our interpretations of what we hear and see them saying and doing. We no longer filter our perceptions and reactions to the other person through the lens of love and the truth of God's Word but through the eyes of our own bitter-root judgments, soul wounds and failed expectations in the relationship.

When we do not see the other person with compassion and forgiveness, we judge them and bind them into our self-righteous and skewed perceptions. They resist being held in this unlawful place of being judged, not by love, but by fear. They react, giving place to the devil who then uses their offense at not being loved and treated with respect and dignity, to retaliate. This retaliation opens the door for them to use witchcraft and manipulation to protect themselves against us and 'get even'.

Relationships are the first place from which our most serious offenses and difficult trials arise. Our own needs for love and affirmation make us vulnerable to other people's sins. Both being rejected and refusing to be loved have created the cauldrons for witchcraft and the crucibles for injustice in which many loving and hopeful relationships have been destroyed. Like two unmovable boulders, fear of love (rejection) and fear of forgiving (bitterness and stubbornness) have set us up as an enemy to each other.

We have been caught up between being defensive and judgmental, between trying to get justice and justify our actions, all in an effort to prove we are 'right'. To see ourselves as 'right' we have to see the other person as 'wrong'. Carrying a self-righteous opinion sets up tension and division in our relationships and makes forgiveness difficult.

We distrust them and try to get even. We hold grudges and feel both justified and guilty. We build walls and fight back. We blame ourselves and become anxious. We fail to be perfect and feel ashamed. We try to take control in order to manage the chaos of other people's lives only to be swallowed up by it. We become bitter when we are treated unjustly and swallow the offenses. We are tempted to 'stay mad' until the issue is resolved.

Fear pushes us into isolation as pride and religion work to jockey us into a position of power or give us a clever argument to prove we are right. We are offended and we offend. We hurt one another trying to get the other person to admit they are wrong for not loving us. However, even the very act of pointing out the injustice and the offense can make us appear demanding and contentious because true love must be freely given, not demanded. True love is not conditional and cannot be given in response to a demand.

We can also become frustrated and angry when others fail to pay the debt of love they owe us. Instead, out of the counsel of their own familiar spirits, they continue to reject us and send us double messages which bring confusion and more discouragement. In an effort to get love we can sometimes initially put one another on a pedestal. When they fail to be our 'prince charming' or our 'damsel in distress' we walk away confused and angry that we gave up so much of who we are to make them be something God never designed them to be.

We take counsel from our familiar spirits and become discouraged. We become resentful, feel guilty for being angry that we could not be 'good enough' to make them what we needed them to be for us to be 'okay'. We are tempted by Hell's counselors to believe that their rejection of us is 'our fault' or blame them for being insensitive. As the pain and failure deepens, the list of grievances grows. We choose isolation and indifference over love and become bitter and alienated from one another.

EMOTIONAL/ENVIRONMENTAL INVENTORY

- Describe your emotional environment as a child growing

up in 3-4 words: (Chaotic, satisfying, overwhelming, stressful, supporting, abusive, structured, fun, emotional, numbing, terrifying, safe, strict, never sure, frustrating, not fair, busy, magical, great, sad, stressful, dangerous, confusing, frightening, dramatic, peaceful)

- Take the 3 words you used and describe your childhood in further detail using examples: (Frustration is the tug-o-war between 'I've got to' and 'I can't', which sets up the dilemma of the irresolvable conflict. When the issues of the conflict cannot be solved, the result of that irresolvable conflict is depression which often manifests as migraines, stomach aches and digestive issues or insomnia.)
- What were the issues, spoken and unspoken, that operated in your family? (Substance abuse, any forms of abuse, including sexual abuse, rage, anger, poverty, instability, rejection, favoritism, parental neglect, emotional neglect, sickness, death, tragedy, unpredictable behavior from adults, unrealistic expectations, religious irregularities, other)
- Name 2 of the most frustrating things you deal with in your relationships:
- Name 2 ways you deal with those frustration in your relationships

COMMUNICATION

The scripture admonishes us to "let no corrupt communication proceed out of your mouth, but what is good for necessary edification that it may impart grace to the hearers." (Eph. 4:29) It goes on, "Let all bitterness, wrath, anger, clamor and evil speaking be put away from you, with all malice and be kind to one another, tender-hearted, forgiving one another, just as God in Christ also forgave you." How simple is the admonition? How difficult to obey?

The point of communication is to build relationships. Communication, from God's perspective, is the sharing of words and deeds to bring encouragement, instruction, correction, edification, and grace. We are told to love one another and it will be enough. All the law is fulfilled in this simple command. If we do this one thing, we have done all we need to do to satisfy every other command. Let the law of kindness be in our lips.

Kindness in relationships is all too rare. What seems to be rare in some has become entirely lost in others; lost among the burdens and baggage of striving and stress, burdens most of us insist upon carrying through life. The dangers of being hurt coming out of rejection and injustice have made kindness a risky option only a few of us dare to take. Caution and the preservation of ourselves have replaced safety and planted fear in the middle of our relationships.

Kindness is the fruit of love, not fear. Kind words and a good report bring health, not only to the bones (Pr. 15:30) but life to the soul. If what the heart is full of the mouth speaks, it only takes a few sentences for us to tell what is really in someone's heart. At least that is what we think. Presumption and silence give the Enemy opportunity enough to bring confusion into our relationships. He can fill the silence with any number of erroneous conclusions.

Kindness dies among the unspoken desires of our broken heart and we live in obscurity, unknown and unloved. Kind words spring out of love for the other person. When we are secure enough in God, we know that we can trust Him to protect us. He gives us the grace to live peaceable with even the most difficult people. Love is the final testing ground for the truth that, "with God, all things are possible", especially when we are closely related to a very difficult situation or person. (Mt. 19:26)

WHAT WENT WRONG? – BUILDING OUR SENSE OF SELF WORTH

The Enemy has set us up to build our self-worth out of how other people respond to us. Though our needs and expectations may not be articulated, when they fail to 'read our mind' and understand what we want, we become upset. This condition promotes anger and conditions us to become disinterested in paying the debt of love. Retaliation and hurt convince us to withhold from others that which is rightfully theirs, which in turn, makes them angry. Failing to give each other the love and forgiveness they need breaks the Lord's commandment to 'love one another'.

If the list includes baffling and unclear responses from the recipient of those messages, is it because you may be sending them a double message, one that is a mixture of truth and lie, or could be taken two different ways. Is the request impossible to respond to because it is loaded with confusing directions or contradictions or anger? Are they being 'passive aggressive' in setting you up to entrap you and give themselves a clever 'out' to justify themselves of any wrong doing? Are they filtering your kindness through their own system of fear and hurt which distorts your intentions and breaks down relationships? Have your responses to your people become rote and automatic? Are you reacting out of old opinions or keeping a long list of past offenses? Are the decisions you are making coming out of learned behavior or are you being guided by the Holy Spirit?

- Are you sure that you are speaking with integrity and your messages come out of good intentions and acts of kindness? Are they being correctly perceived and received by the person you are sending them to?
- List the responses you are getting from the one you are trying to communicate your love to: Remember, what the heart is full of the mouth speaks. Be honest with yourself as you ponder these questions.

HURT PEOPLE

There is an old saying that says, "Hurt people hurt people." Hurt people are difficult to live with. They are touchy, defensive, withdrawn and controlling. They exploit their relationships to extract for themselves what they perceive to be needful to preserve their own life. All that is holy and true is at the mercy of one who does not hold love to be precious.

They use and abuse the gifts and good will of those around them feeling fully justified in doing it, not suspecting it to be a mark of selfishness and the operation of the unloving spirit. Difficult and hurt people come into their relationships with a consumer mentality to take and not give, to buy and not share, to gain whatever they need to build higher walls and bigger castles to protect themselves.

The devil has twisted our relationships into blades that poke and words that provoke. He has conditioned us to live in our human nature even after we have been made free to live in our divine nature. We use our experience to build filters through which we see those around us. We perceive reality through the events and our perceptions of those events. If our experiences are full of hurt and condemnation we will begin to see the world through eyes of pain and failure.

THE BODY'S FILTERING SYSTEM

God's filtering system is faith. The devil's is fear. In the Word of God, He instructs us to 'meditate', to ponder and turn over in our minds, "whatever things are true, whatever things are noble, whatever things are just, whatever things are pure, whatever things are lovely, and whatever things are of good report". (Phil. 4:8)

As we meditate on things that are 'praiseworthy and virtuous', there are enzymes produced in our brain that cement the things we are thinking about into our long-term memory bank. These things then become part of the 'faith filter' through which we see future incoming information and stimuli. These new bits of information are interpreted through past experiences. If those experiences were positive and hopeful, we are persuaded to proceed in faith and respond in the Spirit.

Faith bridges the gap between where we are stuck and the promises of God, and carries us past the fearsome guards and gatekeepers of this present reality. It allows us to enter into and abide in a new place prepared for us by the Spirit, a place of freedom to change and seeing even the impossible through the eyes of the possible.

The same filtering process works in reverse when we think on fearful things. If the new information coming in through our senses is processed and viewed through a filter of fear or trauma it will send a message of alarm to our body. When fear interprets the information as dangerous, the hypothalamus sends a message that alerts outlying members of our body to prepare to defend or protect themselves.

When we meditate on lies and negative outcomes, we give place to the spirit of fear that perpetuates pessimism and hopelessness. The things we fear the most, as Job observed, come to pass because we have given those thoughts the power to influence us. Since both fear and faith demand to be fulfilled, the one that will prevail is determined by 'whose report' we choose to believe - fear or faith? The Enemy's projects his fear onto us. The temptation to fear must be specifically resisted, not just passively accepted and ignored. Passive agreement with the devil is still, in his book, an agreement!

The 'fear filter' interprets our relationships through past experiences and negative outcomes, coloring new information with distrust and suspicion. Fear makes recommendations to the mind based on past experiences that sounds the 'flight and fight' alarm throughout our bodies to prepare for battle. Many times the fear is subconscious, or irrational. It operates as an unreasonable anxiety that we cannot specifically put our 'finger on.' The signals of alarm send us into biological places of unconscious alert and places of conscious worry.

God intended this 'General Adaptation Syndrome' (GAS) to fuel our systems with high octane fuel in times of crisis to protect and preserve us in moments of imminent danger, like lions and fires. Cortisol and adrenalin were not meant to fuel the regulatory system for normal, everyday biological functioning. When we are afraid of something we cannot psychologically identify and the danger never goes away, we become hyper-vigilant and anxious. This constant state of alarm wears us out and depletes our body's natural defense systems. It also releases too much cortisol and histamine into our bodies. If these chemicals remain in the body for a prolonged length of time, we become toxic and chronic fatigue sets in. Our physical health begins to break down.

Bodies are not the only things that suffer when fear dominates a relationship. Things that should be simple become laboriously difficult. Words are misinterpreted. We are misunderstood. Feelings get hurt. Emotions escalate. Defensiveness steps in. Control gets us to try and make the other person do what we perceive to be necessary for our safety or stop doing what is hurting us. The power struggle ignites a war. The war draws the battle lines, often with the help of a human court system. Lives are torn up. Dreams die. Worlds are shattered. Children are lost. Hope goes away.

- Identify the seniores that ignite fear and tension in you that make you anxious.

COMMUNICATION IS

Relationships are, in essence, the words and thoughts you express to another person. Communication, the sharing of information and feelings, is at the core of every relationship. The quality and depth of our communication can vary and are determine by the perceived level of safety we have in sharing with the other person. SAFETY is the most basic and important element in both communication and in building loving relationships.

If we do not feel safe and accepted, we will limit our vulnerabilities by withholding information about ourselves from the other person. Our level of satisfaction in our relationships is directly related to the honesty and the level of freedom we experience in our communication with the other person.

There are basically four different levels of communication. The first and lowest level, considered the least risky revolves around sharing information regarding non-personal topics. The weather, the latest TV show, or sports are all considered as safe subjects, (unless, of course, you are passionate about your favorite team that just lost the big game and someone else is glad they did).

This second type of communication is called 'reporting the facts' and is usually practiced to probe the safety limits in our relationship with that other person. If the depth of intimacy with the other person does not change over time, even as we get to know them better, we settle into a comfort zone of superficial, non-confrontational information sharing. We are afraid to hurt the other person's feelings and just 'don't want to rock their emotional boat'. This is a common ailment in shallow communication and keeps our relationships from going deeper and growing into more spiritually mature experiences.

The third level of communication begins to explore feelings and thoughts. Feelings and opinions open up another 'can of worms' which many people are afraid to deal with and often seek to avoid. Again, the issue is safety. Fear says: It is not safe to say anything because the other person might react or get mad. If things are not safe, we learn to settle for just not talking about certain things.

Feeling 'unsafe' leaves many issues unaddressed and many lies un-confronted. Being defensive and taking things personally opens the door to offense and shuts the door to deeper relationships. (The key to not getting defensive and offended is to know who you are and where you came from.) A defensive response in either person says more about them than about the other person. Taking things personally and getting offended is one of the biggest obstacles to having good relationships.

The fourth level of communication includes the expression of our own thoughts and inner feelings, ideas, and wishes. We will not move into the deeper level of communication unless we feel safe. The issue of safety cannot be over-emphasized in having good communication. Good communication is the key to good relationships. It is the mortar that holds together the individual bricks that build the foundations and support systems for healthy individuals, families, communities and civilizations.

Safe means it is okay for you to say what you are thinking and feeling. It lets us be ourselves without fear of being judged or disregarded. Only those who are secure in who they are and are not afraid of being judged or falling into the trap of judging others can survive the rigors of deep and meaningful communication. Only those who value the truth above their own opinion and need for personal safety can become defenders of the truth and enjoy the freedom of speech as God intended it.

Communication often has a text as well as a subtext. The surface message may be presented as the topic of discussion, as expressed in words, but the hidden agenda, often expressed in the body language, may contain what is really on our mind. The agenda is hidden because it may not be perceived to be safe to be brought out in the open. We sometimes 'test the waters' with jesting and making a joke about something when rejection or disrespect is the real, though hidden, point of the message.

Sometimes to avoid conflict, we will deny any other message is intended than the one that is being sent, when, in fact, the hidden message expresses our true feelings and thoughts. The reverse of deciphering the hidden messages can also be true. The message can be misinterpreted to mean something that was not part of the sender's original meaning allowing conflict and accusation to break out into judgment.

Communication can be full of words that judge another. We consider our perceptions to be a true and accurate interpretation of the other person's intentions and 'judge' them according to our own standard of right and wrong or personal hurt and offense and not according to God's standard of love. Fear of being judged presents a huge obstacle to sharing openly with another person. If we do not feel protected and accepted by their love we will remain silent, hidden and emotionally unavailable to them.

Fear of rejection, lack of confidence, the need to control what people will think or want, all influence us to avoid and conceal the truth about the issues we do not want to deal with in the open. Without honesty in our relationships, however, we really have no relationship at all. Our relationships are only as real as we are. If we lie to the person we are in relationship with and refuse to be transparent, we are kidding ourselves to think we have a solid relationship with them. If the apple is half rotten, the apple will soon be all rotten.

If fear continues to manage our interaction and interprets the messages in such a way that nothing is ever said clearly, it will ever be truly understood. If fear is not dealt with, nothing will ever change for the better for long, the relationship will always be strained. The strain creates pain and discouragement. When our relationships are not feeling good, we no longer want to be in them. If the communication does not change, the relationships will not be healed and the pain will not go away.

COMMUNICATION PROBLEMS

The Bible teaches us to "let your 'yes' be 'yes' and your 'no,' 'no', for whatever is more than these are from the evil one". (Mt. 5:37-38) Paul elaborated on Jesus' command to speak clearly and decisively. "When I was planning this, did I do it lightly? Or the things I plan, do I plan according to the flesh, that with me there should be yes, yes, and no, no?" (II Cor. 1:17-19) "For all the promises of God in Him are yes, and in Him Amen, to the glory of God through us." (II Cor. 1:20)

Being afraid to speak the truth for fear of 'rocking the boat' or not defending it for fear of what others might think compromises our identity and the word of God. Telling people what they want to hear and not saying what they need to hear are both very serious forms of lying and idolatry. They will catch up with you in the end, even if you are trying to justify your words as 'being nice or cooperative' or wanting to 'keep the peace'. The only way we can truly be intentional and honest is to "speak the truth in love" (Eph. 4:15) so the one who hears can "grow up" in Christ.

When Jesus taught His followers not to 'swear' He was not just referring to using bad language or cursing. He warned us not to make promises we had no power to keep. He does not want us to 'beat around the bush' in dealing with each other, but to be open and honest. How many of our conversations and lives would change if we just did that one thing different?

- It's time to 'say what you mean' and 'mean what you say'. Many of us are in the habit of telling people what they want to hear. Describe your tendencies in answering a matter.
- Are you afraid to tell them what they need to hear?
- What is something you need to correct in your communication with another person? Do you love them enough to tell them the truth?

A TIME TO SPEAK

The Bible tells us that there is "death and life in the power of the tongue."(Pr. 18:21) There is a time to speak and a time to refrain from speaking. (Ecc. 3:7) Wisdom, as given by the Holy Spirit, is the only way we can know what time it is. Many of us are trying to 'hear' what the Spirit is saying to us because we try too hard to figure out what God wants. God's will is not a puzzle that we have to decode. God's will is clearly demonstrated in His Word as taught to us by the Holy Spirit. The pressure is clearly on HIM to lead us into all truth. How hard is it to follow Him and be a branch abiding the Life GivingVine?

Identify how many times in one day, or a week, you have experienced one or any of these. Write the number behind the phrase (if you can).

- You 'beat around the bush'- you didn't let your 'yes' be 'yes' and your 'no' be 'no'
- Fear of what 'they' will think
- People pleasing, afraid to speak the truth
- Compromising values to avoid arguments with others
- Not feeling heard
- See your words getting twisted
- See others projecting their stuff onto you
- See yourself as being unjustly blamed and falsely accused
- See yourself as being lied to, used, and taken advantage of

What are the lies you believe that sustain these patterns?

CHAPTER 7

MY RELATIONSHIP WITH MY SPOUSE

Marriage is meant to be a holy union between a man and a woman given as a picture of the love and kindness Christ has for His church. God uses their covenant relationship to build a safe house for the nurturing of children through the consistent impartation of the Word of God. Marriage is the means God uses to build the family and to protect it from the generational curses of injustice and the patterns of iniquity that have been passed down through the bloodlines.

This makes marriage a primary target for the Enemy's brutal assaults especially against the women because of the curse put upon them for Eve's independent action to eat the forbidden fruit without consulting Adam. As a result, the Lord said to the woman "your desire shall be for (toward) your husband and he shall rule over you." (Gen. 3:16) The Law of Reciprocity was in full effect. Now the woman who had acted without her husband's approval would be seeking his approval for everything!

The woman who had been given as a helpmate to her husband was now saddled with a desire to please and do for her husband, the one who had now been given the authority to rule over her, as he saw fit. Think of the implications for evil that were released in this decree. Adam was mad at Eve and blamed her for the terrible thing that had just happened. From now on everything she tried to do to be helpful would be looked on with suspicion and met with resistance. Her actions would be misinterpreted as manipulating or controlling and she would be seen as inferior and weak. The very one who was to treat her as his own body would despise her and many times, hold her back from being able to fulfill her destiny in the things she had been designed to do.

It was easy for the Enemy to get her to feel rejected and treated as untrustworthy. Her influence would be marginalized and her safety would be compromised. Adam was tempted to write her off, not as "flesh of his flesh, and bone of his bone," (Gen. 2:23) but as an object of contempt to be ruled over and refused. Anger and blame from her husband reduced his delight and desire to treat her kindly. He was tempted to become bitter against her. She had been deceived and was to be blamed. The Enemy presented her to Adam, as spiritually inferior and competitive, to get him to treat her like an enemy and discard her influence.

Satan saw danger in the intimate power and potential for strength God had built into the union between Adam and Eve when he saw God take her, not from the common clay, but from Adam's own body! His only hope in dividing the house of mankind was in splitting up the union between Adam and the wife he dearly loved.

The Enemy's goal was more than accomplished when he got Adam to blame both God and the wife "You gave me" (Gen. 3:12) for the sin. The pattern of this curse of bitterness between husbands and wives is still upon those who do not understand the original ramifications of that curse, (which is most everyone). Although the curses have been officially broken by the death of Jesus who became a curse for us, we do well to claim those freedoms because God wants to act on our behalf to set us free. He never intend for this curse to be used by the man to justify abusing and despising his wife any more than God intended for the Enemy to use it to break up marriages.

Because our first parents were both corrupted by the fall, the result was not pretty. No longer was either one that interested in surrendering themselves to the other in the loving trust of a covenant relationship. As can be seen today, there are many more marriage based upon the idea of a pre-nuptial contract than a God ordained covenant. (Contracts are written to protect our assets from being stolen from us by the other party. Covenants are made to share those assets with each other).

As a result, both men and women continue to suffer the violence of the Evil One as he inflicts the pain of these bitter root judgments upon them and their marriages. Combining the vulnerable disposition of marriage and the fear of being controlled, with the critical task of raising children makes doing relationships within the family even more difficult. The destruction of families and the continued reinforcement of the 'body of death' are a primary focus of the Enemy who uses marriage as a device to separate relationships and steal souls.

CONTROLLING OTHERS

When we only feel safe if we can make our environment and the people in it do what we want them to do, we are not internally secure in who we are. When we are insecure, we try to control those around us. When we cannot control them, we become frustrated and angry. Of course, they do too. It's not fair or right that they should have to yield their life and free will to us because we want to have our 'way'. Some will submit to that kind of tyranny for a while, but sooner or later, it goes bad and backfires.

Trying to control others is frustrating and exhausting because they have a mind of their own and may be trying to secure their own physical and emotional environments to feel safe. In either case, someone has to give in or forgive in order for the relationship to survive. If neither one is willing to let the other be free, a decision to break the relationship is often made. The decision to divorce is painful, but since a marriage must have the cooperation of both persons, when one abandons it, the marriage is in serious danger of being over.

Intimidation, anger, irritation, threatening, projecting guilt, manipulation and control cause very upside down and dysfunctional relationships. When the person we are with is insecure and angry, or has unresolved issues of self-worth, they will spend their emotional energy trying to prove their worth either by justifying their behavior or by trying to gain the approval of others. This makes them even more vulnerable to rejection, failure and lying.

When we try to fix each other by controlling them and they do not appreciate it, we become resentful. Fear is twisting our relationship into something it was not meant to be. We become angry and upset when they do not do what we want. We try to manipulate the situation so things do not get worse. We do not know when to let go. Frustration becomes normal and we believe our mate is just being rebellious or ungrateful.

Those with a more pious disposition adopt a more religious position in the battle for control and survival in their relationships. They cling to the traditions of their childhood churches, find fault, blame others and preach the Bible to cause their mate to submit by making them feel bad or guilty. Adding religious obligations to the control package increases weight of burdens already too grievous to be born and brings the wrath of God upon those who would use His Holy Word for their own unholy purposes.

SILENCE

When we seek approval from a source outside of God, we are being set up for failure and will be disappointed. As we withhold information and withdraw ourselves emotionally from the relationship, distrust and stress begin to build a wall of unresolved issues around us. We provoke a fight to justify our getting offended and mad, so we can walk out. Or we shut down to protect our position to avoid a conflict. Nothing ever gets settled because no one is willing to admit to the truth or change to align themselves with the truth.

Holding back information by keeping things inside is used to gain and control the informational advantage over the other person. Not answering simple questions in an evasive, passive-aggressive way does not promote safety or respect, nor does it open up healing dialogue between two people. When we self-protect and keep the other person guessing about what is going on, we have the control. When we use control to keep them from getting the advantage over us, we are operating in fear and not love.

Getting the 'silent treatment' sets up a resignation that leaves us feeling like we have no options except to go away, believing 'there's nothing I can do about it.' We feel helpless and angry for be treated with such disrespect. Our hearts also become hardened against asking for forgiveness or admitting we are wrong. Fear of being judged as weak or ridiculed as stupid keeps us from admitting wrongdoing lest we be seen as the guilty one.

Turning to silence is one of the most effective ways to both control another person and to prevent resolution. The power of silence opens the door wide for the Enemy to put any 'spin' on the situation he desires and offense becomes the narrative as things get quickly spun out of control. He is given the power to fabricate all manner of innuendos and fearful thoughts to fill in the blanks until we are worn down with troublesome misperceptions and evil imaginations. Pride and fear rule the day leaving us no hope of discussion, expression, or resolution.

DON'T LET HER WIN

Another strategy for handling disagreements is the stalemate. What happens when my need to vindicate myself conflicts with your need to be validated? Do I go huffing and puffing and storming out of the room, throwing a fit to cut you off? Or do I intimidate you into agreeing with me through bullying and coercion or withholding from you that which is rightfully yours? What happens when pride and stubbornness and fear and the need to be right prevail, even when we know we are wrong?

After a while, hardness of heart sets in. When that happens I no longer 'hear' the whispering of the Holy Spirit to my spirit. I am no longer plagued by the minor irritations of my conscience or moved by the pleas for mercy. If I refuse the love of the truth in my life, God will send, allow or permit, a 'strong delusion' to take over my mind and convince me I am right and all is well with my soul, when it is NOT! (II Thess. 2:9-12)

The argument, 'If I give in and admit she's right, she wins', has kept countless destructive and unnecessary fights going on for years. Many think that if they keep resisting and rebelling against the word of correction, she/he doesn't win. Neither one wins in this battle for the 'last word'! Nor can I stay in control of my miserable life or 'win' by talking myself into choosing the thing I know is wrong, in order to win.

O foolish man! We do not win until we receive and embrace the truth. If we are bound together in a covenant of marriage and have made a vow to each other, witnessed to by God, we are one flesh. To cut off our mate's life from our own is to despise ourselves. (Eph. 5:28-29) We would be miles ahead if we knew that when love wins we both, all, win. This principle of winning can be applied to any type of fight where the point of contention and the need 'to be right' are not as important as to love.

REBELLION

Rebellion is as the sin of witchcraft. Witchcraft is tapping into, or seeking help from a power source other than God's. That power source often becomes identified as 'me' or, 'It's up to me.' 'I've got to do it myself' and 'I've got to take care of myself,' become the mantra of the fearful. We reason that our survival reduces down to me taking care of myself. When life is unstable, we fail to find people in our world who are trust worthy, who will treat us fairly and care about us enough to get to 'know', love, us. We feel vulnerable and rejected. The pain of that rejection makes us feel alone, unworthy and unlovable.

When children live in unpredictable and dangerous situations they perceive to be rejection, they often learn to take care of their own needs themselves. Rejection opens the door to being tempted to take Rebellion's suggestions to ease the pain by adopting an attitude of independence and indifference. If 'I don't care', then what you do to me won't hurt. The Enemy's solution to pain seems reasonable enough to the child – 'that if I can't feel it, it won't hurt', right?

Rejection and pain create insecurity. Insecurity is the fertile breeding ground for rebellion, control and manipulation. Many of those who practice witchcraft and manipulation also see themselves as 'abuse victims'. These patterns of abuse create strong feelings of hatred and contempt which come from feeling rejected and unloved as children.

When truth is not spoken in love, the child fails to 'grow up' properly (Eph. 4:14-15). When children are not nurtured in the love of their parents, trust and reliance upon the Lord are not correctly instilled in the child's heart. Fear takes over. When we do not see God as adequate or available or interested in us or our needs, we fall into the temptation of becoming bitter against God and to take matters into our own hands.

Even if the child is taught about God, the Word of God itself is often both mis-taught and misunderstood. Their concept of God becomes skewed by their misperceptions and those of their teachers. They may see God as angry and hard to please. They may see the hypocrisy of their parents in saying one thing and doing the opposite, or even worse, making excuses to justify contradicting their own words and actions. Eventually, they will find themselves playing the hypocrite they judged their parent for being.

Hypocrisy causes children to try and resolve the perceived discrepancies in their family by making adjustments in their own thinking to resolve the conflicts they are feeling. Somebody must be wrong. It must be my fault. They become confused. For some, the remedy seems to be to try harder to 'be good'. Others get 'mad'. Ultimately many of them are being set up by the adults in their world to believe God is mad at them for breaking the commandments and they are turned away from the truth.

When the parent uses the Word of God in an unjust and manipulative way to 'guilt' and 'control' their children, the child is taught to follow after a counterfeit gospel based upon 'keeping rules' and 'being good'. If they do not suspect they are being taught the wrong gospel, and if they fail to keep the strict standards often presented as 'Christianity', which they will, they become discouraged. The fruit of the counterfeit gospels are to 'feel guilty', 'get mad', 'give up', and 'go away'.

If they choose to stay in the 'church' in a climate of spiritual error, where the counterfeit gospels are preached, they will begin to 'gossip'. To justify their behavior they begin to compare themselves to one another. Judging themselves as better, more righteous than others, the spirit of hardness of heart and spiritual blindness will set in. None of these responses are the fruit of the Gospel of Jesus Christ because they do not reflect the true Gospel of Jesus Christ or fulfill the great commission.

Legalism and religion put an impossible set of rules on our children. They are taught to believe they must be good and stay out of trouble to make God happy. These are deadly deterrents to knowing the truth about the goodness of God and the Gospel of Jesus Christ. They set up a perfect storm in the child's soul. They feel rejected and cut off by God for not keeping the commandments of a gospel that turns out to be false. If they come up against the hypocrisy of the church, they are seen as rebellious. If they submit to the false gospels, they become bored and angry for being lied to. All of religion's design is to alienate them from the One True God. They become prime candidates for the shiny lures of sin and reckless abandon. The Enemy has done this to separate all of us from the truth of the Gospel of Jesus Christ and the love of the Father.

The dangers in resisting the counterfeit gospels which we have come to believe to be the true gospel are subtle. Our children are labeled as rebellious. Those who drift away from the church are called 'backsliders'. All of them go searching for 'another gospel' or another way to find peace and be empowered. Witchcraft is waiting in the wings along with new age paganism. Rejection alienates them from their parents and the support of the church. Cooperation and unity within these dysfunctional and dishonest relationships becomes impossible. The child becomes skeptical and disinterested, bored and sedated. They become drift away from their families. Their pursuit of good behavior is traded for finding acceptance in joining another collection of similarly minded disenchanted seekers. When truth is traded for the lie and loving, caring relationships go away and the love of many grows cold. (Mt. 24:12)

The emotional void is filled with more, 'I don't care' and 'you can't make me'. These are two of the often-heard statements are from the spirit of rebellion who has come in as a demonic solution to the child's pain of rejection. Pain comes from the guilt of failing to get their parent's love or acceptance. They reject their parent's lifestyle. Rejection has set them up to fall into the grip of rebellion.

Rebellion offers those who practice it the promise of freedom from the control of others. If that control is emotional, which it often is, 'not caring' disconnects the child from the pain and disapproval of rejection and hurt. The Enemy's solution of 'disengaged disinterest' provides some temporary relief from the pain for the one who heeds its counsel. If 'I don't care what you do', 'what you do cannot hurt me?' This strategy, however, brings no lasting solutions for peace and restoration without the gift of repentance. Repentance means to change your mind and turn around. Repentance and confession of the agreements made with the lie are critical for the deliverance of both the parent and the child caught in the demonic snares of rebellion, witchcraft, addiction and rejection.

THE STRONG-WILLED CHILD

Distrust and fear are the spiritual roots behind the manifestations of rebellion in a 'strong willed' child. They do not believe or trust in anyone or in anything except what they have experienced and determined to be true for themselves. Rebellion works well with the spirit of fear, the initial subconscious, demonic, body-of-death programming we experience in the womb. That same spirit of fear begins to craft our first experiences as we come into this world and launch out into life.

Infants, young children and teens are most vulnerable to the Enemy's suggestions because their identities are still soft and as yet unformed and uncertain. They are not secure in their identities. Stubborn, autistic and strong-willed children are insecure children who have been born with a spirit of fear. They do not know who they are, nor can they trust those around them. As a result of that distrust, they insist upon controlling everything and learning everything for themselves, which often turns out to be the hard way.

The strong-willed child insists on being taught by their experiences and the circumstances rather than by listening to their parents or taking their instruction from the experiences of others. They are actually being set up in opposition to others because they have been set up in opposition to themselves. This makes it difficult for them to believe others or to submit to authority for fear of being deceived or controlled.

There are different kinds of rebellion - the obvious outward, active, verbal resistance and the silent, hidden, compliance that looks like cooperation. Those caught up in a more silent, inward type of rebellion begin to live an independent and solitary life-style filled with all manner of dangerous spiritual and psychological detours and mental constructs. They lose contact with the truth of who they are in order to take on a pretend personality that they can hide in.

Fear and Rebellion teach these children to build a fantasy world of their own, a private little world where they are empowered and have control over things. In the autistic child, for example, everything must be done the way they want it done or they 'freak' out. Anything they do not want cannot be in that world. Everything must be in its place for them to feel safe. Their world must stay 'undisturbed' so they can stay in control to be okay.

NARCISSISM

Rebellion sets up the fearful child to be feel vulnerable and isolated, distrusting and insistent. One who is bound by or influenced by a spirit of rebellion and feels like he/she has to protect themselves will reject the influence of others in order to stay safe themselves. They yield to a 'protector demon' that impersonates them to themselves and offers to keep them safe using persuasive self-talk like; 'I don't trust you', 'I'll do it myself', and 'You can't make me'. These response/attitudes cause the child to grow up believing, 'I want what I want' and 'you must do things my way'.

Although the dictionary defines narcissism as excessive self-admiration and self-centeredness, for our purposes we will expand the definition to include a deep seeded bondage to fear that manifests as a more exaggerated sense of self-importance. They also display a lack of empathy, a constant need for attention and praise, fantasies about power, and a sense of entitlement, along with a history of exploiting others for personal gain.

Narcissism's sense of entitlement blinds the person to their own flaws. They have grown up reacting to the way they were raised to embrace a more controlled and exacting view of life and relationships. The original conditions of insecurity and feeling unsafe have morphed into a psychologically ruthless disregard for the life or the well-being of others. Though the Bible does not specifically use the word narcissist it gives the perfect example of one in Nabal, Abigail's husband who is described as a scoundrel whose name means fool. (I Sam. 25:25)

Abusive relationships of every sort, whether they be sexual, emotional, psychological, or physical all begin in childhood with taking down the child's innate sense of safety and innocence by exposing them to difficult and unresolvable situations. The child is bullied into believing what is not good is their fault and they accept the blame assigned to them by the Accuser rather than attribute the failure to an Enemy who is controlling the adults in their lives.

As the child is learning that their life is not safe, because the adults in that world are not trustworthy, they begin to listen to an inner counselor they believe to be themselves. This counselor from within is the spirit of the Enemy that dressed himself in the clothes of 'reason' and begins to coach the child about what they have to do to survive. Using the 'solutions' of this 'inner voice' brings them into a psychological, spiritual snare, though the origin of this advisor is hidden from their understanding.

The spirits of fear and insecurity manifesting as a need to control have begun their covert construction on the citadel of Narcissism. Towers of the 'Self-preservation' and 'Me' (the Protector Demon) who speaks as that inner voice are setting up strongholds to keep out or lock up trespassers, anyone who dares venture into their world. Their castle becomes not only the person's own prison, but the potential penitentiary for any future mates and their children. Evil has set its foot into the 'strong man's house' and the plundering of eternal souls has begun. (See Mt. 12:29 & Lk. 11:17-26)

The Enemy counsels them to 'hide out' in their own little world. Because they have learned it is not 'okay' to be themselves, they learn to pretend to be someone else to protect their real 'self' from being exposed. They agree to bury themselves, at least for a while, until it is safe to come out. This buried 'self' that gets lost in the charades of pretending, must be found before any true or lasting deliverance can be had for those bound by the spirit of narcissism.

These children learn to perform even as they are learning to disconnect from their own feelings. Their own feelings must either be concealed or denied in order for them to survive the pain and confusion of growing up in a dangerous environment. Fear and trauma deceive the child into believing self-preservation is of the utmost importance. This makes lying acceptable and concealing the truth about who they are even more important. God's truth is absent and fear rules their actions.

They begin to build a world where no one is allowed in who cannot be trusted. And since no one can be trusted, these children grow up very alone and isolated. Only those who are willing to keep the 'rules' are permitted to enter their world. As a result, love is rendered as a mechanical compliance and relationships are performed as a matter of rote learning, rather than emotional nurturing and maturation. Perfectionism and performance put upon the child an unnatural and critical expectation of themselves and others. Love is seen as conditional and something that can be manipulated.

Adulthood is a continuation of the psychological distortions gathered in childhood. The person himself is often completely unaware of his/her demands as being unusual or unreasonable. The world they created as a child to survive the craziness of their relationships with the adults who raised them sets them up to live in a distortion of reality. Being controlled by fear and persuaded by denial that allowed them to fabricate their own private world as children now develops into the world they continue to build and control as adults. What started out as a pretend world to make their real world more tolerable has now become authenticated as rigid and right.

The belief system and agreements that govern the narcissist have allowed the Enemy to build and imprison them in a stronghold they are willing to defend as if their life depended upon it, because, in fact, they believe it does. Usually the narcissist is unable to empathize with the feelings or be sensitive to their mate. An element of 'disconnection' and 'disassociation' blocks the narcissist (the one being held hostage by fear and trauma) from realizing or recognizing what they are doing.

Fear and pride use a spirit of disassociation to keep the one bound by a spirit of narcissism from seeing a need to repent. Without the revelation of Jesus Christ, and His truth, there will be little hope for change or freedom for the narcissist or the person, spouse or child, bound in a relationship with them. Operating under this kind of fear and the need for self-preservation, the narcissist sees nothing wrong with what they are doing.

Using their own basic parameters to define the world, the narcissist is a super controller whose demon has a diabolical skill in the art of manipulation. For those who claim to be Christians this includes the use of a legalistic, religious terms and interpretation of the scripture to hold others in check. Because the Enemy is very clever, he will often mix large dose of 'religion, law keeping and submission' into their relationships to insure an ample supply of the guilt and confusion necessary to control and manage those caught up in a narcissistic relationship.

Covering the relationship demands with legalistic, religion expectations creates even more condemnation and confusion in the one(s) being 'gas lit' or 'brain washed'. (Understanding narcissism is also foundational to understanding cults because many of these super controllers also end up being cult leaders).

Inserting the works of the law into the mix makes it easier to build a case for guilt and fault finding and harder for those in relationship with the narcissist to discern what is really going on. The victim is blindsided by the wiles of the Enemy and fails to understand the deadly spiritual stronghold they find themselves locked into. The perpetrator must have everything and everyone who is part of their world behave in a certain way in order to be safe. By the time this thing is over, both sides are blinded to the violations they are making to the commandment to 'love your neighbor'.

Being in a personal, primary relationship with a narcissist is extremely difficult and can be fatal. Domestic violence, sexual abuse, and rage are initially hidden to the naïve and unsuspecting, often concealed by their opposites. Although the narcissist may appear to look like a wonderful father, mother, husband, wife, pastor, or person in the community, the truth is, behind closed doors the opposite is true. This makes being rescued from an abusive relationship with a Narcissist even more difficult because no one believes the victim is a victim.

THE NARCISSISTIC MARRIAGE

Initially, for those venturing into a marriage with those being controlled by a spirit of narcissism, all appears to be good. As someone approaches the castle of the Narcissist they have hope of being loved, well taken care of and maybe even rich. Anyone who marries a narcissist will be obligated to conform to the spirit of fear that controls the narcissist. These are the unspoken rules of the stronghold the narcissist lives in.

One of the most deadly thing about walking into a narcissistic trap is, not only is 'love blind', but that there may be only a few 'red flags' waving their warnings in front of their castle. Many of the initial feelings of hesitation are covered over by the charisma, flattery or religious language that persuades the soon-to-be mate to disregard the warning signs and marry the person of their 'dreams'.

The fairy tale ideal of living in a beautiful castle with the prince of her dreams presses the woman to allow herself to be pursued. She believes whoever rescues her from the dragons of fiery family relationships will be her prince charming. Her eyes are filled with Cinderella visions of hope and happily ever after. Her desire to be a 'good' wife and mother sets her up to try harder to make everything perfect. When her husband gets upset she is tempted to take the blame and feel guilty. When she is rejected or criticized by him when things go wrong, she makes excuses for him and submits to his demands, at first.

Satan uses her desire to submit to God and please her husband as a perfect recipe for disaster. Submission and accusation can turn into 'gas lighting'. (Gas lighting is a slang term for making someone feel like they are the crazy one and whatever is going wrong is their fault). Worn down by the 'brow-beating' and 'put downs' of the narcissist, the one controlled by the spirit of narcissism, usually the wife, will eventually begin to physically and mentally 'fall apart'.

Her body and soul get sick and serious physical conditions like cancer and the autoimmune diseases begin to erupt. The bonds of trust and safety have been broken and the physical body takes the ultimate brunt of the impact. The woman's health is being offered as a sacrifice on altar of marriage. The Enemy is using the marriage vows of 'until death do us part' literally to bring death and separation to the unsuspecting couple.

As things deteriorate in the relationship the life of the hopeful one begins to grow dim. They are barraged, day after day, with the moods and demands of the one they chose to believe loved them, the one they wanted to spend the rest of their lives with. At first their minds offer them other explanations for the pain and difficulty they are experiencing. They do not suspect that they are being manipulated by the one they love because they are constantly being told they are the reason for the other persons unloving behavior.

As things progress they become increasingly confused into believing the problem is 'all their fault'. They have been programmed to believe that 'if I had just been a better wife'; a more 'obedient child'; or a 'better Christian,' things would have been fine. The victim has been trained to assume the blame and responsibility for the behavior of both members of the relationship.

The primary requirement for anyone entering into a relationship with a narcissist is submission. To the unsuspecting and naïve, surrendering to what looks like love and devotion, including keeping the vow to 'love and cherish until death do us part', becomes the golden noose around their neck. They do not realize they have both boarded the train to Auschwitz, and the train is moving. In some cases, tragically enough, death through abuse finally does part them!

Jesus warned us to not make vows or enter into oaths for a reason. He said in Matthew 5:33-37 to let our 'yes' be 'yes' and our 'no' be 'no' because 'whatever is more that this is from the evil one'. Couple the power of those vows with the idea that God hates divorce leaves many people feeling completely trapped and compelled by God to stay in their deadly marriages. Yes, God hates divorce, but He hates what divorce does to the members of the family even more. He hated the destruction that was being perpetuated upon those caught in the grip of the Evil One. That is why He gave the people a "certificate of divorce" because of the "hardness of their hearts". (Mt. 19:7-8) God never intended for us to throw wisdom and discretion out the door in pursuit of love or relationships. If anything, wisdom and discretion are crucial in the formation of good, solid relationships. Let us therefore, discern when it is time to speak or be silent, to stay or to leave.

The goal of the narcissist is to get his wife to submit and become completely assimilated into his narcissistic world, the world he built in his childhood and has lived in ever since. Unaware of this agenda, the woman pursues the relationship with another goal in mind. When a woman is persuaded to say 'yes' to the man's proposal, she has, in effect said, 'yes' to whatever he wants to do to her, be it good or evil. Of course, no one is forcing her to marry a narcissist, but the true nature of what Hell has planned for them is hidden long enough to lure them both into its strangle-hold.

The demon in charge of keeping the vow is now using their vow to justify the accusations he is bringing against them. When the physical body cannot continue under the oppression of submission-at-any cost, it begins to break down. God never intended marriage to be a divinely sanctioned arrangement for the enslaving of His daughters by His sons, or vice versa. (There are just as many horrific situations where men are entrapped in the grip of a contentions wife (Pr. 19:13) who may, knowingly or unknowingly be practicing witchcraft against him. Both are under the sway of the "terrible one" (Is. 49: 24-25) and are being used by the Enemy to destroy each other along with their precious offspring.

The spirit of injustice thrives in the presence of the spirit of oppression. Injustice and offense give way to anger. Anger is the external evidence that a crime has been committed against the law of love. When the law of love is violated injustice and offense begin to break down the relationship. The emotional distress gradually gives way to the spirit of infirmity which works to tear down the physical health of the weaker one.

The spirit of infirmity now takes center stage which creates a twist in the relationship. The narcissist, who has been held under the counsel of fear and aggression, is now fully engaged in seeking a mental or medical intervention for their spouse. They go to the doctor or to the therapist to get treatment and medication to fix what is, in reality, a SPIRITUAL problem. As the narcissist begins to care for the sick one he is seen as the 'good guy', who looks like a 'saint' for being willing to 'put up with' and 'take care of' such a difficult, sick person (the one who had been gas-lit and made to look crazy).

This reinforces a spirit of self-righteousness in the narcissist and brings more mental confusion to the targeted person as public sympathy increases for the abuser. Deception and spiritual blindness set in as the narcissist is tempted to believe they are helping the afflicted one and have done no wrong. Spiritual blindness also causes him to see no wrong-doing on his part. He sees his intentions as good and himself as righteous, when, in fact, he/she needs to confess their sin against the law of love. They are deceived into believing they care, when, what they are doing is intensifying their control of the other person. The real roots of the problem of fear have not yet been addressed. Both are completely unaware that the spirit of divination is fully in charge of this train wreck in the making.

Few suspect that the original roots of the sickness they are both now dealing with were caused by the spirit of fear and narcissism, which is a form of fear and control. Fear has opened the door to the unloving spirit who has opened the door to hardness of heart and rejection. Sickness and disease all come from and are sustained by violations committed against the law of love. Guilt (over sin) and confusion (about worth) set up the torture rack that pulls the afflicted one apart. Denial and accusation and the stubborn refusal to repent and admit wrong doing have now trapped both the abuser and the abused, making them victims of the same Enemy who is systematically using them to destroy each other.

As they begin to hate and judge one another, the Devil sets up a wrestling match between flesh and blood. The Bible says, "For we do not wrestle against flesh and blood, but against principalities, against powers, against the rulers of the darkness of this age, against spiritual hosts of wickedness in the heavenly places." (Eph. 6:12) How many couples would ever suspect the troubles in their marriages, including the idea that sicknesses and diseases are due to the manipulation of the hosts of wickedness in heavenly places? The only effective remedy against this spiritual take-over is to know the truth of who they truly are in Christ and the true nature of spiritual warfare.

THE BODY DOES NOT LIE

To be effectively controlled by someone the person's spirit must be broken. If the one entering into the stronghold is not aware of the rules of the controller, that the one entering into the citadel of the narcissist must conform to the dictates of the original occupant and submit to his\her demon controllers, they will eventually be destroyed.

For someone caught in a narcissistic marriage, (both men and women), there are basically three options, and two ways of escape. The first escape is to leave, usually through divorce. The second is death. When the wife cannot endure the oppression any longer, and stops seeing herself as the 'crazy' one she is faced with a hard decision. She can leave, but if there are children and no financial means to support her, leaving may be almost as difficult as staying.

If she seeks the Lord and finds her strength in Him, she may decide her life is more valuable than to be lost and swallowed up by the spirit of narcissism, repression, cruelty, coercion, sickness, persecution and condemnation. If she sees herself as lovable and worthy of love, she will have the courage to leave. It is for this very reason, that God gave us the permission to divorce, though He hates it because of the damage it does to those involved. Divorce is like amputating the leg to save the life. He is our healer in every situation of the life, and the healer of the broken heart.

The second option for someone caught up on the citadel of narcissism is to stay in the marriage and pray for the husband/wife to get delivered. In this option they take the risk of becoming weary and losing their own identity in the relationship. The revelation of Jesus Christ and His truth make the way for deliverance through godly sorrow, repentance and confession of sin the only godly solution. Confession of sin that comes through the revelation of Jesus Christ is the only way to true freedom and healing in the narcissistic relationship.

Many choose to stay and try and work it out without deliverance. They stay for the sake of the children. They give up their lives for the sake of 'peace and quiet'. They become passive and depressed, hoping for nothing more than to satisfy the demands of the spirits that control the narcissist. They essentially lose their hope and quality of life, and become spiritually unfulfilled and physically sick. They are swallowed up and over powered by the fear that controls the one who lived in the stronghold first.

In the second option, if the spouse agrees to remain under the control of the narcissist, (as stated above) the physical body of the victim will begin to get sick, giving way under the pressure of the psychological and emotional abuse. In the case of all illness and disease, though we may have been lying to ourselves and believing those lies for years, our bodies do not lie. Though they can become confused, as indicated in the manifestation of a compromised immune system, our bodies know the truth. Our tongues may lie but our body does not lie. The body is saying 'cannot do this any more'.

When our body is constantly hearing the 'put downs', it becomes confused about our 'goodness'. Our immune system, which is designed to protect us, becomes double-minded and will become compromised. A compromised immune system opens the door to sickness and disease. When we are subject to a steady diet of negative words; guilt, shame, rejection, and condemnation make us feel bad. We get sick. When negative words are spoken over us, our body reacts by pulling down the natural physical protections that maintain health and we will see our body 'turn against itself'. (Pr. 15:30)

For many women who decide not to leave, getting sick, or even committing suicide, eventually present themselves as escapes from the stronghold of narcissism. Once they have a 'nervous breakdown' or get cancer or an auto immune disease or some strange undiagnosable syndrome, they no longer feel responsible for what happens. They give up on their life and their hope and trade the pain of rejection for a disease that will eventually release them into death. As the couple begins to slip under the control of the Evil One, they are both victims of the Enemy's destructive circumstances and evil snare.

The third option many use in seeking to overcome or survive a narcissistic marriage is to practice witchcraft against the narcissist. Practicing witchcraft is like fighting fire with fire, fighting control with control. When the law of love is broken many feel justified in getting justice by their own means. Anyone who practices witchcraft, however, is also breaking the commandment to "love your neighbor as yourself" (Gal. 5:14)

Anyone, but especially women who turn to witchcraft to get the 'upper hand' , or get even, are insecure and most likely reacting to having been rejected and abused by a man first. The Enemy uses control to create a hatred of men which provokes these women to trust no man, do it themselves and take control. He gets them to believe that they are 'victims', then empowers them, through witchcraft, to fight back. This then allows the Enemy to come in and 'save' them from their 'evil' husbands. Everything gets so twisted that few ever realize what the devil has done to divide the house and destroy all the precious souls that live there. With the Enemy running what looks like a 'supportive world system', the lies confusion broadcasts are sustained through resistance and offense. Reconciliation give way to division and the conquering of marriages, families, societies and the human body. Jezebel was a perfect example of this kind of manipulation and contempt in a wife. (I Ki. 16:31)

Now both spouses have become an equal match in the destruction of the other. They define and maintain their relationships and the way things work, either with force or flattery, using charisma and bullying to play psychological games on each other. No one is any longer innocent, naïve, unsuspecting or in control. As lavish and intentional as the original wedding ceremony might have been, there is no longer any desire or ability to share their lives together or honor the spirit of love in holy matrimony

FEAR – THE ABSENCE OF LOVE

If we refuse or fail to receive godly instruction and correction growing up, and if we refuse to receive wise counsel, either because of distrust or fear of losing our freedom to 'do it ourselves', our life and the lives of all those around us will be hard. When things do not 'go right' we will blame others and make excuses for our own uncooperative behavior. Control and manipulation become justified. Anger mounts under the weight of perceived injustices and relationships are broken.

Life is the place where love and fear meet and make war. It is the co-mingling of the two most powerful and compelling forces on earth. The battle between the two is a battle to the death, with the stakes being the eternal souls of men and women. God's remedy for sin is repentance and confession, forgiveness and humbling of ourselves. If we want to get back to the place of truth, we must do it God's way. All other ways lead to the pain and destruction.

The Bible tells us "Faith works by love." (Gal. 5:6) The absence and opposite of love is fear. Fear works by doubt. When I doubt God's goodness and His faithfulness to provide for me, I fall down under the circumstances I find myself caught in. I feel overwhelmed. Lies overtake truth and I am brought into bondage. Love and fear, rise up out of truth and lies. The battle between the two creates the storms of life. Much like hot and cold winds rise and fall, and blow through our lives, they create 'turbulence' and unrest. When love and fear clash, the pressure rises and we are forced to choose what we believe. Are we going to go with fear or are we going to stand with faith?

While some may rest on the balmy beaches of ease on the sunny side of life, most of us struggle with the waves whipping up on the shore. Every one of us has more than our share of difficulty in life. Some of us are living in a perpetual hurricane where fear creates severe disturbances of the soul and tornadoes destroy life without warning. We panic and try to control our circumstances and use our relationships with others to create a shelter in the storm.

And, just as we cannot control the storms on the beach, or the weather in the sky, there are many things, especially in other people, that we cannot control. In those moments of fear and vulnerability the Enemy comes in to offer his support. His favorite method of operation is to divide and conquer, to set up the difficulty and then come in to solve the problem he provoked in the first place. Using this Hegelian Dialect approach allows him to come in disguised as a benefactor, and uses our dependence on him to gain permission to take over our free will and control us.

We are only preserved from his treachery by the watchful hand of God. He keeps us steadfast, and anchored in His truth and love. God's goal for every storm is to cause us to know He is with us in the boat (Mt. 8:23) and will keep us from death. We can know that Christ dwells in our hearts richly through faith and He will root and ground us in His love. (Eph. 3:17)

LOVE IS

Love is not drama or a Hollywood movie, though Hollywood has made much profit out of the drama of love. True love is not a fairy-tale story of prince charming coming to the rescue of the damsel in distress or a box of chocolates that sets us up with an expectation for a romance and excitement that our experiences cannot match.

Love is not a list of ten ways you can serve me, or a simple solution to paying the rent. It cannot be taught in a class as it is more lived than learned. It can as often be found in a concentration camp in the grip of suffering as in a diamond ring or a million-dollar mansion.

Love is the currency of heaven invested in earth. Love is patient and kind, and believes for the best. Love is an action, not a feeling. Love promotes being known and validated. It protects, keeps us safe in the care of the One Who loved us from the beginning. It brings acceptance by and appreciates as precious and irreplaceable the one who is the object of its affection.

In business we have contracts and agreements written out to describe what is fair; what you will do for me and what I will do for you. It guarantees legal protection should injustices occur. Love is not like that. Love loves, whether it is loved back or not. "But God demonstrates His own love toward us, in that while we were still sinners, Christ died for us." (Rom.5:8)

LOVE IN MARRIAGE

Love is not always a 50/50 deal in marriage. It is not always an 'even' trade and a mutual exchange with both parties in full agreement and total commitment. In love and marriage there are vows and covenants, but no guarantees of agreement over the middle line. Love promises to pay the debt and be there in whatever circumstance, faithful in every trial. That is why love is so coveted and sought out.

But that is also why love is so difficult and vulnerable. It takes the risk of being taken advantage of and rejected. It suffers from the possibility of being maligned. Only with the love of Christ will one who stands willing to be faithful without an escape clause, be able to stand. Even if the loved one leaves, love does not act out of hurt, betrayal, abuse or take advantage of its commitment for selfish gain.

Fear is the antithesis of love because "perfect love casts out fear." (I Jn. 18) Fear brings torment that acts out of anticipation of lack, and fear of harm. Its major response comes out of self-preservation. 'I will reject, hurt, distrust, push away, take from, and control you before you can do any of those things to me because my life comes first because it is all about 'me' and what I want'. These are not the words of love.

Love builds no walls and sets no limits because its protection and preservation are not an external event but internally secured. Love is a way of being that says, 'you' are more important than my comfort or temporary gain. Love will remain even to the day that we will be in His company and see Him face to face.

Love is being trained by and for the purpose of perfecting and advancing the potential and best interests of another. Even as there will never be an end to God Who is love, there will never be an end to the opportunities He has given us to love one another in this place.

LOVE NEVER FAILS

The essence of love is acceptance. Love overlooks a fault. Love is a call to action. Love is the fulfillment of the commandments. The Bible says, "Love never fails." (I Cor. 13:8) But what happens when love does fail? When people in our world walk away and we are left alone, unwanted, and unloved?

Walking in the spirit of this world creates a futility of the mind and a darkening of the understanding that alienates us from the love and life of God. Through ignorance our hearts become hardened. We move in our relationships with our feelings and our love begins to fail. Fear replaces kindness and great suffering fills the hearts of both the innocent and the offender.

Because of lawlessness, the love of many grows cold. (Mt. 24:12) When love fails, fear captures us and we live in the bleak, dirty, dead winter of its grasp. God again wants to heal our hurts and warm our souls with His love through the love of others. He is the Good Shepherd who makes us lie down in green and gentle pastures, beside still waters.

Why would we choose to live a life of lawlessness, under the counsel of unkindness and do each other such harm? How do we think that depriving another of their rights to life, liberty, and the love of God will somehow insure the successful pursuit of our own life? How can we live with ourselves numbed out and shut down to the needs of others, living selfishly and cold-hearted, without conscience; unresponsive to the cries of the children when we were once children ourselves?

The only answer is not a very good one, if it is simply that we do not know any better. Fear sometimes presents itself as the 'tough guy,' that provokes us to take action and find a solution. We intimidate others and bully them. We tell lies to cover our true intentions and our sins. We lie to ourselves to justify our actions. Soon we begin to believe the lie is the truth, and lying becomes a way of life. We lie to each other and think nothing of it.

A relationship based upon lies cannot be a true relationship nor will that which comes out of it be genuine. Those relationships based upon lies will be pseudo-relationships based upon pretensions and deception. When we present a false front and deceive the one we are in a relationship with, the fruit of that relationship will be false and unfounded. It will be a plastic imitation of the real and unable to nourish our souls or knit our hearts together in love.

When we lie to someone we are telling them:

- We do not respect them enough to tell them the truth.
- We do not value an honest relationship with them.
- We will take care of ourselves first.
- We are using them for our own gain.
- We do not love them.

When we refuse to pay our debt of love to one another, we have sinned against the 'law of love'. Anger and injustice rise up between us because we were not given that which is right and just and is rightfully ours by divine design. God created us worthy and precious. His creation of us has justified our existence on the planet. He death qualified all of us, whosoever will, to be partakers with Him, in His Kingdom. In return He expects us to give to one another that which He has so freely bestowed upon us.

Love cannot be earned or gained as a prize for a contest won. Love can only be love when it is unconditional, and freely given. "Therefore put away lying, (and let) each one speak truth with his neighbor, for we are members one of another". (Eph. 4:25) Right and satisfying relationships begin with putting away fear and lying, and speak the truth with one another.

It takes courage to speak that which is true and honest when fear of being ripped off, or fear of rejection and fear of being judged and ridiculed stand in the wings of your mind and heart waiting to condemn you as a fool for being so loving. However, it is not man's approval we seek or fear of his disapproval that we seek to avoid. To love one another is the will of God and great blessings accompany it!

Wars and fights have never been able to settle matters of the heart. We lust and murder, and covet, and try to establish boundaries to get what we think we need or want to be happy, only to violate the law of love. When we try to get our needs met at the expense of another person, we withhold the love that is rightfully theirs and steal from them that which is not rightfully ours. Boasting, bragging, bullying and refusing to submit to the truth are the work of fear, pride, insecurity and control. When fear wins over love, insecurity prevails against faith and love's victory is lost to the lie.

LOVE SUFFERS

Most of us look for ways to get out of suffering. We try to feather our nests and secure our future. Love suffers for Christ's sake, "For to you it has been granted on behalf of Christ, not only to believe in Him, but also to suffer for His sake." (Phil. 1:29) Love believes that "the sufferings of this present time are not worthy to be compared with the glory which shall be revealed in us." (Rom. 8:18)

Love does not behave rudely and even when treated that way, does not take things personally or get offended. It is dead to the evil intentions of others and overcomes evil with good. It passed the test and allows God to examine its heart and check its motives for faulty values and weak connections.

It causes us to endeavor to be like Jesus and forgive even as He did. Love overcomes bitterness and resentment and though love may suffer many things, it never suffers regret for making every one precious. Love loves. Love understands we killed the Son of God out of ignorance and realizes many still do not even understand any of that. Love still waits for us to admit we were wrong, 2,000 years ago that we might receive forgiveness for our sins and deliverance from the Snake Pit of life.

"And this I pray, that your love may abound still more and more in knowledge and all discernment. That you may approve the things that are excellent, that you may be sincere and without offense till the day of Christ," (Phil. 1: 9-10). Love takes advantage of its opportunities to love and as long as we have lost no opportunity, we have lost nothing.

Make your own list of reasons for not loving your neighbor, whether that neighbor is your wife, husband, child, children, co-workers, boss, pastor, pastor's wife or political leader or enemy.

We do not enter into the place of love because:

- We are afraid we will get hurt and be rejected.
- We are self-absorbed and too busy.
- We are distracted.
- We get offended and take things personally.

Relationships fail when:

- We isolate and withdraw from others out of fear.
- We do not take the time to know someone.
- We do not let someone else know us.
- We do not consider love the solution to the problem.
- We refuse to be reconciled.
- We want to stay mad and offended.
- We hold onto anger as part of our identity.

Relationships work when:

- We know who we are and love ourselves.
- We let go and let the other person be who they are called to be.
- We help them become all they can be.
- We know 'what time it is' in applying God's wisdom to the need.
- We pass the love test and keep looking for a way to love in spite of resistance.

DOING RELATIONSHIPS THE RIGHT WAY

Reconciliation does not begin with the other person. It always begins with us. If we know someone has something against us, we are to go to them (Mt. 5:23-25) and agree with them "quickly" while we are still on the way lest they take us to court. If, on the other hand, we have something against someone else, we are to take the initiative to go to him or her. "If your brother sins against you go and tell him his fault…" (Mt. 18:15).

Reconciliation begins with releasing the offender from your judgment. Forgiveness means you turn the crime over to God and release the person from your judgment to let God be the judge. True justice is impossible to obtain without forgiveness and the intervention of the righteous Judge.

Judging is not the same as discerning the fruit. Jesus said "Do not give what is holy to the dogs; nor cast your pearls before swine, lest they trample them under their feet, and turn and tear you in pieces." (Mt. 7:6) Identifying the nature of the man and the quality of his fruit is not forbidden. Jesus said, "By their fruits you shall know them." (Mt. 7:16) "For out of the abundance of the heart the mouth speaks." (Lu. 6:43-45) By their deeds we will know others. Even delusion and deliberate deception cannot mask the fruit that comes from them.

We must become fruit inspectors, not judges. Many of us think injustices cannot be corrected unless I take up the offense and correct the matter ourselves. We do not need to judge something for justice to be served. Bitterness and condemnation step in front of peace and reconciliation making love and forgiveness even more difficult. Love overcomes fear through our trust in God, the Righteous Judge, to make things right and bring justice.

Make a list of the injustices you've suffered and people you need to forgive.

POWER IN FORGIVENESS

For many of us, forgiveness is a worn out subject. We have heard it a thousand times, but still are not sure we have forgiven or if we need to forgive again. The difficulty comes when we think forgiveness is based upon a feeling. If I still feel 'mad' at the person, I will be tempted to feel like I have not really forgiven them.

The truth is, forgiveness is not based on a feeling. I can forgive someone by an act of my will, just like I get up in the morning when I do not feel like it, or do the dishes when I do not feel like it. The task is done by an act of my will, not by how I feel about doing it or how I felt when I did it.

Forgiveness is everything, especially to those who think they deserve none. Forgiveness is hope. Forgiveness is God's number one requirement in our dealing with each other and in His dealing with us. All have sinned. There is none righteous or any better than anyone else in the category of sin. All of us fall short of the glory of God. He who would have mercy, must give mercy. For any who want God to forgive them, they must first forgive.

In some relationships, forgiveness may be needed many times a day, not because we did not forgive right, but because new offenses are coming to light. How many times do we have to forgive someone? Peter's question was not only genuine, but also telling. He thought there was a limit, a number that would fulfill the quota of good deeds and right actions that would exempt him from further obligation to his naughty neighbors. That is why Jesus cautioned him that he might need to forgive someone 490 times in one day, if necessary. (See Peter's 7x70 admonition on forgiveness) (Mt. 18:22)

Our question may not be much different from his. How many times have I told you? What is my obligation to the unlovable, the wicked, and the difficult ones who make my life miserable? What is my obligation to the scoffers, those who deliberately hurt me; who steal my life or my wife and steal that which God has given me, to consume it upon themselves; who withhold from me that which is rightfully mine; those God is using to "perfect that which concerns me" (Ps. 138:8) and make me more like Him?

Our forgiveness is not based upon the other person's changing or asking for forgiveness. Our forgiving them is not invalid if they do not change. It still counts even though they continue to sin against us. Forgiveness is, however, the only thing that can help them change. Jesus gave us great power and a great privilege to forgive others in John 20 when He said, "If you forgive the sins of any, they are forgiven them; if you retain the sins of any, they are retained." (Jn. 20:23) He has given us a tremendous responsibility and privilege to release others from the grip of sin and condemnation and lift them into the place of forgiveness and restoration.

Not forgiving someone the Lord is admonishing us to forgive is like agreeing with the devil that they should not be released from their sin or the consequences of it. How many times have we needed forgiveness ourselves? And how many times have we felt condemned because others withheld their forgiveness from us? Remember Jesus simple words to those ready to stone the woman taken in the act of adultery, "Let him who is without sin among you cast the first stone". (Jn. 8:7)

Forgiving others is an essential key to getting forgiveness and justice for ourselves. Whenever we present our 'case' for justice before the Court of Heaven, we are in essence, turning the crimes and injustices committed against us over to the Judge. Forgiveness is releasing someone from your judgment and allowing God to be the Judge. Forgiveness is submitting the injustices we have suffered over to the Righteous Judge. When we turn the crime over to the Judge of all the Earth, we are assured of a fair and just settlement in the restoration of the freedom that has been stolen from us and our descendants.

* * *

M ost of us live with no real or true idea of who God is or what His heart is toward us in this present "evil world".

Jesus came as the express image of His Father to 'show and tell' us how the Father felt about us. Trying to discern God's true intentions through the crazy, chaotic circumstances of spiritual warfare as waged every day in the midst of us makes it almost impossible to discern the true nature of anything including our relationships. That is why Paul admonishes us to, "judge nothing before the time, until the Lord comes, who will both bring to light the hidden things of darkness and reveal the counsels of the hearts; and then each one's praise will come from God." (I Cor. 4:5)

Many of the questions we entertain in our minds and hearts are subtle suggestions from the Enemy who would like to divide our affections and set up confusion about any number of things in our lives, including our relationship with God and the acceptance of others. Guilt is one of the Enemy's most effective methods to get us to carry the responsibility for the things we have done under his influence. Repentance and confession are God's remedies for healing and forgiveness in the matters of sin. We do well to heed them.

So how do we discern who speaks and who is acting in our lives? Are the words we are believing from heaven or hell? Does reducing the words and thoughts down to their 'lowest common denominator' reveal peace or anxiety, or love and rest, or fear and striving? Is the fruit good or bad? Does Jesus love me? Is the Bible an irrelevant and out dated book of fictional history, or does it contain the words of life?

WHEN WE SEE JESUS

When we look at Jesus we see God. When we see how Jesus treated people, we get a picture of how He feels toward us. In that He is still alive and lives forever, and in that He never changes, we can know that His attitude and thoughts toward us are the same as we see them to be with those He touched in person over two thousand years ago.

When we look at how Jesus did relationships we find a man who was just and righteous. We see a Man not tainted by religion or blinded by self-righteousness. We see a Man who did not need the approval of men. He knew the fickle, movable, indecisive nature of man and thought He did not rely on men, He did not despise them or base His worth on their opinion of Him or take His direction from those around Him. (Jn. 2:24-25)

He was not 'too busy' to bless the children or 'stop' to call for blind Bartimaeus. (Mk. 10:46-52) "He wept" with Mary. (Jn. 11:35) He came for Jarius' daughter, (Mk. 5:35) and laughed with His disciples. He comforted the widow of Nain and helped Peter pay his taxes. He rested in the very midst of the storm and drank water drawn for him by the woman with five husbands. He took nothing for Himself, including the glory, and though He did not even have a pillow for His head, He had everything!

He treated people with compassion, knowing their oppressed and condemned state. (Jn. 3:18) He treated people with dignity knowing that they had been made in the image of God. When the woman was taken in adultery and Jesus had a chance to demonstrate to the world His disgust for such blatant sin, He forgave her and passed by the opportunity for judging her and gave it to others.

With gentle authority He told the Paralytic he was a 'son' and his 'sins were forgiven'. (Mt. 9:2) What remarkable power! What kindness! What hope and forgiveness He gave to those who had none. Why should they be anything different from what their circumstances told them they were, if there was no hope of knowing they were loved? When all their trying had only ended in a pathetic life of isolation and shaming, He gave them a reason to live.

Out of His poverty, many became rich as He gave them everything they needed to live in peace with God. He forgave the bloody, dirty, dying thief on the cross next to Him and did not force those who would not hear, to come. His 'yes' was 'yes' and His 'no' was 'no'. He told it like it was and did not mince words, backtrack, apologize or feel sorry for Himself.

He was even patient with those whose hearts were hardened and set upon silencing Him. He identified them as hypocrites and enemies of His Father's Kingdom. "You are of your father, the devil" and "white washed sepulchers." (Mt. 23:27) He told them the truth, if perhaps they would heed Him. He did not look to others for endorsement and asked very little for Himself.

He is the role model, par excellence, for how we are to be in our relationships with each others. He sent the Holy Spirit to prepare us, to teach us, and to make us more like Him; to guide us and lead us into all truth and the freedom it brings, that there would truly be no question, that whom the Son sets free, is free indeed.

He was hungry and alone in most of what He did, more often misunderstood, than understood. He did not become bitter, or resentful at the injustices He suffered, nor did He retaliate. He fed the followers and carried their pain, and left judgment to His Father. He forgave those who called for His descent from the Cross, refusing to be shamed by their ignorance. (Heb. 12:2 and Lu. 23:34-35) He laid down His glory in Heaven to become one of us to teach us how to do Relationships God's Way!

* * *

CHAPTER 9

THE SET UP PRAYERS

These 'set up' prayers have proven to be invaluable in providing protection for us and our families as we enter into spiritual warfare in behalf of others and ourselves. We cannot emphasize enough, the importance of using these prayers or ones similar, regularly, especially at the start of every new day and every time you begin a counseling session. Each word has come to have significance although these prayers are only a model of how to pray. You can surely pray your own prayers using your own words. Nevertheless, under all circumstances, we urge you to prepare each time of ministry by taking the time to pray.

Dear Lord Jesus,

I thank You, Lord God, for this day. I thank You that You are the God of Heaven and Earth and that you are in control. I thank You for this place and I ask You to fill this room with Your peace, Your power, Your protection and Your presence. I ask You to seal the perimeters of our time and space this day, with Your precious Blood, that Your will be done here, on earth, even as it is being done and declared in heaven. I bind the operation of the Enemy and forbid his attempts to confuse, confound, disrupt, interrupt, distract, hinder, delay, conceal, steal or resist the work and revelation of Jesus Christ in this place.

(Prayers for the one being prayed for)

I ask You to tuck _____ into the palm of Your Hands, that they will feel Your peace and sense Your presence, and hear Your voice. You said, 'My sheep know My voice'.

I bind the powers of darkness arrayed against _____ and forbid them to call for reinforcements to the strongholds or to network with those in the strongholds. I bind the strong man, the familiar spirits, and any who hold assignment over _____. I forbid your operations against _____ . I render you powerless and inoperative, and command you who keep the strongholds to prepare to leave the temple dwelling place of the Most High God in _____. I command that the Light of Your Truth and the Sword of Your Word, Lord God, make manifest the hidden works of Darkness, and separate them from every part of _____ and us.

I also pray for divine favor, that the Blood of the Lamb cover each one of us, our families, those who pray for us and work with us and have come to us for help in the past. I pray for those who love us, and for protection of all that pertains to us and them. I pray that You would keep us in our words, our conversations, our relationships, our communications, our thoughts, and our perceptions, that the Enemy cannot get into our lives to bite, divide, devour, destroy, deceive or separate us in our fellowship with each other or from Your love, Lord God.

I pray that we would all rightly divide Your holy Word of Truth, and that the thoughts and meditations of our hearts would be acceptable in Your sight. I declare, according to Your Word, that "no weapon formed against us will prosper" and that any curse that has been sent against us, either in word or deed, made either ignorantly or intentionally, will fall to the ground and be covered by the Blood of Jesus Christ, that the Enemy cannot use those words against us. I pray that those who have cursed us will be blessed with a deep and holy revelation of Your truth that would set them free.

Your Blood cancels out the agreements and contracts my generations past have made with the Enemy. I declare his continued operations in my life through those lies to be illegal. I command that the familiar spirits who works through those agreements to be separated from me and my descendants and their lies be exposed by the light of Your truth. I also ask that You would give us a deeper revelation of Your truth and keep us in good health. Watch over us and keep us safe. Keep us from the hindering spirits and make the thieves put back all that they have stolen from us. Cover our vehicles, our travel, our finances, our property and the work of our hands, that we might enjoy the fruit of our labors. Let the gifts of Your Holy Spirit work freely in and through us that we might be used to make disciples and bring the good news of rescue and salvation to those lost and hurting.

I thank You, Lord Jesus, that you are the Wonderful Counselor. I ask You to come now to give us Your Spirit of wisdom and revelation in the knowledge of You as we cry out for discernment and rest our hope fully in You. Amen.

PRAYER FOR FORGIVENESS AND RELEASE FROM SELF-HATRED AND SELF-REJECTION

Dear Lord Jesus,

I come to You right now and ask You to forgive me for rejecting, hating and despising myself. I ask you to forgive me for the judgments I have made against myself under the counsel of shame and fear, in listening to the lies of the Devil. Forgive me for using his description of who I am to describe my life. Forgive me for using his counsel to guide my life. I ask You to forgive me for believing him instead of You. I cancel out all of those agreements made with the Enemy against who You say I am and ask you to remove all the judgments I've made against myself in listening to him and have mercy on me.

I ask You to take the Sword of Your Truth and remove from me all of Satan's demonic judgments and the consequences of those judgments the Devil has made against me for judging myself. Remove from me all the judgments and consequences of the judgments I have made against myself including agreement with the spirits of fear, self-preservation, self-reliance, self-hatred, self-rejection, self-judgment, self-destruction, self-condemnation, condemnation, doubt, self-doubt, guilt, shame, pride, self-righteousness, anxiety, perfectionism, failure, death, infirmity, chaos, confusion and unforgiveness toward self. I ask you to give me a deep revelation of Your love for me and peace in my relationship with You and with myself. Thank You, Jesus.

PRAYER FOR SELF ACCEPTANCE

Dear Lord Jesus,

I come to You right now and ask You to forgive me for rejecting and despising myself. I repent. I come before You to declare, before heaven and earth, that I have changed my mind and repent of embracing the lies the Devil has formulated against me. I refuse to believe the liar and his lies any longer. I choose to release and forgive myself for despising and hating the creation You brought forth when You made me. I choose to live and breathe and have my being in You and give You glory. I choose to let Your Holy Spirit reflect Your image in and through my life and conduct. I agree with the instructions You gave my body to "live". I no longer choose death.

I take authority over my body, mind,(thoughts,) heart,(emotions), which are known as flesh, and in Your Name, Lord Jesus, I command all liars, deceivers, destroyers, and every spirit of confusion, and rejection that operate in my body, mind, heart, soul, will, emotions, and spirit, and all that pertains to them, to leave me. I am the temple property of the Living God and will have no fellowship with the hidden works of darkness! I ask You to forgive me for hating myself and opening the door for the Enemy to bring his judgment against me using my own words to do it. I choose to live and ask You, Lord Jesus, to cancel all vows, words and death wishes I uttered against myself in wanting to die.

I ask You to bring forth Your image in me and reflect Your purposes in and through my life. Loose me from judgments I have held against myself in listening to the counsel of the liar who uses those judgments to get me to sabotage my own life by holding me in unforgiveness toward myself. I choose, by an act of obedience, to forgive myself even as You have asked me to forgive others. I come to You, Lord Jesus and submit myself to Your care. I yield myself to Your workmanship and commit my salvation to You for safe keeping.

Thank You, Lord Jesus, for making me, me. I am Your idea, and I come into full agreement with Your idea for making me who I am. Thank You for making me just the way You wanted me, and for placing me in time and place as You desired. You are the Potter and I am the clay. Let me be satisfied to be a vessel made in Your Honor and fit for Your use. Thank You, Lord Jesus for this life. I give it back to You. Fulfill all the destiny and dreams, and all Your purpose and desire for my life in making me, that I may, on that Day, hear You say, "Well done, good and faithful servant, enter into the joy of your Lord." Amen.

PRAYER FOR FORGIVENESS OF OTHERS

Dear Lord Jesus,

I come to You right now and choose, by an act of my will, and with my heart, to forgive _____, for the crimes they have committed against me. I release them from the judgments I have made against them and forgive them for their failure to love and protect me. I forgive them for the betrayal and the injustices they committed against me. I release my case against them and the injustices they committed against me, to You, Lord Jesus, and the Court of Heaven. I ask that You would consider my complaint and bring forth a righteous resolution and a just settlement in this matter in favor of truth, justice and mercy.

I ask that you would bless both of us with a deeper revelation of Your love for us. If the person being forgiven is deceased, we ask that God would give their descendants a deeper revelation of Your truth. I ask that You would release me from all the judgments and the consequences of the judgments that have come upon me and my descendants because of any unforgiveness, bitterness, or anger I have held against them. Release me from becoming like the thing that I judged and hated in them.

I pray that You would release me from all the judgments I have made against myself in listening to the lies of the Devil and using his counsel in bringing these matters to justice, including listening to retaliation and resentment. Forgive me for taking things into my own hands and not listening to You. I ask You to have mercy on me, and remove the hurt and pain and confusion and heal my broken heart. I trust You, Lord Jesus, to establish justice and truth inside of me and give me Your peace. Vengeance is Yours and I trust in Your justice. Thank You, Lord Jesus. Amen!

FORGIVENESS OF GOD

Dear Lord Jesus,

I come to You right now and ask You to let me see my true heart. Forgive me for listening to the Accuser who perpetrated lies against You, defaming Your character and identifying You as the One responsible for my destruction. Forgive me for believing his lies about You. I ask You to release me from the lies Resentment has told me about You, and open my eyes to the truth about where You were and what You were doing when the Enemy was raging against my life. Thank you for Your faithfulness to me, and Your Divine Protection in keeping Your promise to never leave me or forsake me. Amen.

WHEN BREAKING OF THE CURSES OF THE GENERATIONS

In dealing with the sins of the generations and the open accounts that have been left standing by those who have gone before you, it is important to understand how the Enemy uses these things to build his case and form his plot against your individual life. When you see the patterns of destruction coming down into your life, you have evidence that what is happening is not a coincidence, nor is it without a design. Recognizing the patterns of destruction removes from us the denial that would counsel us to ignore the obvious and continue to suffer from the curses against our lives that have come from the sins and iniquities of our past generations so we do not continue to live in ignorance. The patterns tell us three things; the plot is not an accident or a random act, it is orchestrated and operated under a deliberate design and intention, and it is predictable.

Once we are convinced that these patterns are real, we will want to take action. The action that must be taken to address the sins of the generations and the "iniquity of our fathers which is with us," (See. Leviticus 26:39) is clearly laid out in the Bible. The first step in breaking the curses and the avalanche of evil that comes down into my life, (even as a believer), and the lives of our children is to: CONFESS THE INIQUITY OF THOSE WHO HAVE GONE BEFORE US. Confessing the sins of the generations, identifying as specifically as possible, the crimes that have been committed, including the very old and unsettled injustices that are still being reflected in the patterns and the offenses we are experiencing, breaks those agreements and voids the contracts the Enemy has been holding over us.

We come before the Court of Heaven to present our case and the crimes that still have not been brought to justice. We ask the Court to rule on those matters and judge the demons that are attached to the ongoing trouble that are coming into our lives as judgments and curse. Forgiveness, releasing that person and the situation from our judgment, is ESSENTIAL in the matter of being released from the judgments either we or our family made against those who sinned against us. Forgiveness is also essential in dealing with the pain and the ongoing destruction of the crimes that have been committed against us. In letting go of our position as judge and taking the position as the plaintiff our requests are clear and the Lord is able to take His place as the Righteous Judge in the matters in which we are seeking justice. This is the only way to get a new judge on the case, the Righteous Judge of all the Earth, who does not at all acquit the wicked.

Those agreements made with the lies by those who have gone before us have allowed the familiar spirits to created particular responses and repercussions in our lives that have brought with them a negative spiritual legacy. Each generation wrestles with the "sins of the fathers" the Enemy tries to carry down on each successive generation. When it is not possible to know the patterns specifically, as may be the case when you are adopted, or do not know what has gone on between your parent(s), the best you can do is confess the general categories of sin and take responsibility to declare them to be an abomination before the Lord.

"But, if you do not obey Me, and do not observe all these commandments, and if you despise My statutes, or if your soul abhors My judgments, so that you do not perform all My commandments, but break My covenant, I also will do this to you: I will even appoint terror over you, wasting disease and fever which shall consume the eyes and cause sorrow of heart. And you shall sow your seed in vain, for your enemies shall eat it. I will set My face against you, and you shall be defeated by your enemies. Those who hate you shall reign over you, and you shall flee when no one pursues you." (Leviticus 26:14-17 NKJV)

"And as for those of you who are left, I will send faintness into their hearts in the lands of their enemies;...they shall stumble over one another,...you shall have no power to stand before your enemies,...your enemies shall eat you up. And those of you who are left shall waste away in their iniquity in your enemy's lands; also in their father's iniquities, which are with them, they shall waste away." (Leviticus 26:36-39 NKJV)

"But if they confess their iniquity and the iniquity of their fathers, with their unfaithfulness in which they were unfaithful to Me and that they also have walked contrary to Me,...if their uncircumcised hearts are humbled, and they accept their guilt – then I will remember My covenant with Jacob, and My covenant with Isaac and My covenant with Abraham I will remember; I will remember the land for I am the LORD their God. (Leviticus 26:40-42, & 44 NKJV)

As we see from these verses, the prescription for recovery and restoration is very specific. If we CONFESS our iniquity AND the iniquities of our fathers, which are WITH us and their unfaithfulness to Him, and humble ourselves, and REPENT of our own participation in those sins, God will heal us and restore blessings to our generational line.

REMOVAL OF THE JUDGMENTS

The breaking of the generational curses includes CONFESSION AND REPENTANCE along with forgiveness and the removal of the judgments. After the patterns are recognized and iniquity confessed, the next step is forgiveness. Forgiveness releases the crimes committed against us to the Court of Heaven and closes Satan's case against us. His demand for blood and his claimed right to continue to violate the temple property of the Most High God are rendered null and void. The Blood of Jesus more than satisfies the Devil's demand for our blood and the death of Jesus more than answers the demand sin has made upon our life. Each person can be lead in this prayer individually, or it can be used as a corporate prayer. Let them repeat each phrase after you.

THE PRAYER FOR RELEASE FROM THE SINS OF THE GENERATIONS

The following prayer is a model for dealing with the oppression and bondage Satan has inflicted on you through his claimed rights against you. The first part of the prayer re-establishes the legitimate ownership of Jesus Christ over that area of your life and legacy, including the place the Enemy is contesting and to which he is laying claim through previous activity and agreement. The second part of the prayer identifies and breaks the generational curses. The scripture tells us those iniquities and their continued operation through the generations is broken through confession. Confession releases us from the Enemy's claims and assault, making his operation in our lives illegal. Pray this for yourself or invite the person to repeat after you....

Dear Lord Jesus,

I come to you right now, as Your child, Created in Your image, and brought forth by Your will and truth. I believe You died on the Cross for me and rose again. I believe You are seated at the right hand of the Father, and that you sent Your Holy Spirit to live in me. I am the temple of the Holy Spirit.

I come today as the authorized representative of my generational blood line to do business before the Court of God, to claim my new inheritance as a new creature in Christ. I confess the sins of my generations past - their idolatry and the crafting of graven images, their reliance upon themselves for safety and sustenance, and declare those things to be an abomination and an insult against the Holy Character of our Heavenly Father. I confess their sin in the use of false comforts and self-indulgence, lust, adultery, infidelity, incest, sexual perversions and the violation of the innocent to be an abomination against the true heart of the living God.

I confess the practices of witchcraft, rebellion, control, manipulation, hardness of heart, stubborn resistance to the Holy Spirit, jealousy, insecurity, and relying on the Devil's power sources, as fear and an abomination against heart of the God Who has promised to love and protect me. I confess all bitterness and holding of grudges, resentment, unforgiveness, retaliation, backbiting, hatred, hatred of God, violence, rage, murder, bloodshed, the shedding of innocent blood, pride, religious self-righteousness, greed, covetousness and disobedience as lawlessness and rejection of the goodness of God and contrary to the will of God.

I cancel out any agreements both knowing and unknowingly my ancestors have made with the Enemy of God through the practice of sin or belief in the lies of the Devil. I confess their contempt for the things of God, their deception, and rejection of the truth, doubt, double minded-

ness and unbelief to be sin and abomination against Your Holiness, Lord Jesus. I confess all agreements made with the Enemy under the counsel of the Strongman, the Anti-Christ spirits, or the familiar spirits who have brought these destructive patterns down into our lives, to be sin, iniquity, and an abomination against the Living God.

And even as I confess the iniquities of my ancestors, I repent for my own participation in these things, both knowingly and unknowingly. I ask you to forgive me, Jesus, Son of the Living God. I ask You to take the Sword of Your Truth and sever the cords of iniquity that have bound me and my descendants to these lies and patterns of iniquity. I ask You to break the curses of the words, deeds, actions, dedications, vows, rituals, oaths, prayers, promises, covenants, contracts, symbolic dedications, and every claim made against our lives through blood sacrifices, human or animal. I ask You to remove all demonic programming and the operation of the "body of death" in all parts of my body, soul, and spirit. I ask You to remove all of the Enemy's assignments over my life. Set me free according to Your Word, "Whom the Son sets free is free indeed."(Jn 8:36) Thank You, Lord Jesus for hearing my prayer.

If there is Masonic or Shriner involvement in your bloodlines you may want to give them a copy of the Masonic prayers (liferecovery.com) to pray privately or you may lead them in renouncing the oaths out loud. The first three degrees of Masonry are especially effective in opening the door for physical sicknesses. Diseases like asthma, heart attacks, stomach aches, choking and mental confusion, including inability to concentrate, can all be part of those curses. If Masonry, including participation in the Shriners, or witchcraft or participation in a specific cult has been identified, specific prayers of renunciation are suggested.

It is important for us to know we have been given spiritual authority over the Enemy or he will deceive us into believing we are helpless and at his mercy. It is also important to confess any sins of bitterness or unforgiveness you might be harboring toward family members and strangers. These acts of obedience take away the Devil's claimed rights to judge you for judging others, (Mt.

7:1-2) as well as, secure the restoration of blessings for your life and the lives of your descendants.

PRAYERS TO BREAK SOUL TIES

A soul tie is like having two signatures on one contract. You cannot execute that contract, to sell the house, for example, if only one person is willing to sign off on it. Many times we have formed soul ties with a person through sexual contact, physical or emotional abuse, and or the exchange of experiences, expectations and words. Though there are many legitimate relationships into which we can enter, there are boundaries which must be respected for each person to maintain their dignity and integrity as a person in that relationship.

Putting others in a binding contract through control or intimidation is not what God wants. Fear and control enslave the other person. Being in bondage to them is a form of idolatry. Controlling them is a form of slavery. Ask the Lord if your soul has been inappropriately tied to any person or thing and if so, how. Pray this prayer to unhook yourself from any unholy alliances you may have formed either intentionally or inadvertently with someone that are keeping you from going forward in your life. People who are divorced benefit much from praying this prayer to release themselves and their former spouse from the vows of their marriage covenant. You are merely completing the dissolution of the transactions in the spiritual world that has been recognized in the natural world.

Dear Lord Jesus,

I come to You right now, Lord Jesus, Son of the Living God, and ask You to break any soul ties operating in my life that bind me or restrict me from freely serving You. I do not want my soul to be tied to anyone else but You, so I ask You to take the Sword of Your Truth, which is Your Word and cut the ties that bind my soul to _____. I ask You to release me from any vows, covenants, oaths, promises, expectations and all exchanges between me and _____ and that every exchange made between us will be canceled and all attachments, including the familiar spirits of the keepers of those vows to be removed from us by the blood of the Lamb of God. I ask You to break the soul ties and set me free to serve You.

I give back to _____ right now, by the power of Your Spirit, all the parts of (himself, herself) including all the parts of (his, her) body, mind, soul, will, spirit, being, expectations, emotions, and circumstances or words and promises that were given to or exchanged with me in our relationship. I also take back to myself, right now, by the power of Your Holy Spirit, all the parts of me that were given or taken in our relationship. I take back to myself, all parts of me, including all parts of my body, mind, soul, will, spirit, being, expectations, expressions, emotions, and circumstances. I ask You, Lord Jesus, to separate me from _____by the Sword of your truth and break the soul ties that had been formed between us. Make me one with myself, and at peace with You. Thank You for setting me free to be the person You have created and called me to be for Your glory. Amen.

PRAYERS FOR THE INTEGRATION AND REUNIFICATION OF THE FRAGMENTED PARTS

After you have mediated the transaction between Jesus and the person who has agreed to allow Jesus Christ to heal (his, her) broken heart you are ready to pray. We ask Jesus Christ to procure safety and establish us in His righteousness. Jesus will give them His peace, joy, eternal life, and the revelation of His truth, etc. in exchange for their broken life. As they agree to the transaction, the deal is done. This is how we pray for them;

Dear Lord Jesus,

Father God, I pray, right now, by the power of Your Holy Spirit, through the Blood of Jesus Christ, Your Son, that You would knit _____'s broken heart back into the fullness of Your perfect plan for (his, her) life. I ask You to reveal to (his, her) heart, the fullness of Your truth in this matter, that they would be free indeed from the pain and hurt and guilt and fear of the past. I command all demonic programming and every system including all back up systems operating under the counsel of Fear that control _____ to be dissolved by the Blood of the Lamb. Amen.

THE PRAYER FOR CANCELING OUT THE AGREEMENTS WE HAVE MADE WITH THE MIXED GOSPEL

Dear Lord Jesus, I come to You right now on behalf of myself, and as the authorized representative of all of my generational blood lines, to cancel out every agreement we have made, knowingly and unknowingly, with the Liar in the mixing of law and grace, and works and religion, which in effect, rejects Jesus Christ as the only Mediator between God and man in the restoration of our relationship with God. I cancel out our agreements with using the traditions of men and good works as a way to get to heaven. I confess our perversion of the Gospel of Jesus Christ, adding to it and mixing it with it, our own ideas of what must be included in His sacrifice to make it complete. I ask you to forgive us for peddling many counterfeit gospels, all abominations before you, Lord God and denying the Gospel of grace and good news as given to us by Jesus Christ.

I reject the crafting of graven images, the practicing of rituals, and religious superstitions that base our righteousness upon our own ability to keep the law as a partial or complete fulfillment of God's commandment. I ask you to forgive us for making salvation something we can or must earn, both of which make You a debtor to us. I ask You to forgive us for substituting programs for the power of Your presence and accepting the doctrines of demons as having come from your Holy Spirit. I ask you to forgive us for using the Gospel of Jesus Christ and the Word of God for our own gain, and as a way to "beat up" and control others who were seeking the counsel and comfort of Your truth. Forgive us!!

I cancel out all practices that bind us to the spirit of man fear or people pleasing in following or preaching a false gospel. I ask you to forgive us for mixing the Gospel of Jesus Christ with the many other things that

call themselves the Gospel of Jesus Christ and are not. I repent for my
own participation in these religious practices and the rejection of God's
salvation. I repent for believing lies and in adding anything to Your
message or method of salvation as necessary to be saved.

I declare that we do not preach ourselves, but Christ Jesus the Lord, and
that our salvation is established through the shed blood of Jesus Christ,
freely given to whosoever believes. I declare that the confession of the
belief that He died on the cross for our sins and rose from the dead and is
seated at the right hand of God, according to Romans 10:9-10 is suffi-
cient to bring us to salvation. I declare "there is no other name under
heaven given among men by which we must be saved." (Acts 4:12).
Amen.

This same prayer can be used for canceling out any other specific
agreements that you find being practiced in your family in regard
to religion, idolatry, and superstitions.

WORDS OF WARNING

When asking Jesus for things do not feel that you must make it
complicated. He is more than willing to help us. The Devil is a
different story. He is very legalistic. With him, it is best to dot the
"i" and cross the "t". Though we might resist the idea of being
that specific in identifying the Enemy, and in dealing with him, it
is necessary to be bold and as firm as possible in naming him. Do
not be double-minded or apprehensive in binding him. (See the
previous things written on the strongman).

Though Jesus has given us power over all the power of the Enemy
and nothing shall by any means hurt us, it is not wise to move in
any kind of haughtiness or arrogance against this foe. He is clever
and you and I, in our human understanding and wit are NO
match for him.

Because the Enemy has gained access into our lives through the
sins of our generations past, it is important that we cooperate with

the Holy Spirit Who dwells in us and get our own lives cleaned up before we start working with others. The Enemy may still have strongholds of fear and deception in us of which we have no knowledge. When you begin to deal with him in others, the Enemy will begin to attack you in some part of your life, if he can. It is best to approach him in this war with the gates of your fort closed and the interior secured. We are grateful to the Lord for His promises and His protection knowing than nothing shall by any means hurt us, as we humble ourselves to do His will. Be blessed. Amen.

* * *

ABOUT THE AUTHOR

Marjorie Cole, founder of Life Recovery, Inc. a prayer and counseling ministry, and author of numerous books, manuals, and cd's has worked as a teacher and counselor for more than 30 years. An excellent bible teacher and conference speaker, she has traveled both nationally and internationally. Her video and audio teachings are seen throughout the world including Eastern Europe, Romania, the African nations, the Middle East and Europe.

Marjorie has worked as a counselor in both Christian and secular settings including Minnesota Teen Challenge where she wrote the book, "Taking the Devil to Court". She has a master's degree in counseling psychology and chemical dependency counseling.

Using a biblical approach to counseling and truth as the basis for freedom, she has developed Life Recovery, Inc., a systematic, comprehensive approach to healing and deliverance that has helped thousands of people apply scriptural principles to their lives, bringing them to truth and a new freedom in Christ. Those principles include understanding spiritual warfare, deliverance, inner-healing, breaking generational curses, and discipleship.

Marjorie, along with her husband Jarry Cole who pastors True Light Church, host Rescue Radio, a weekly podcast. They have been in the ministry for over forty years.

Among the many other literary works by Marjorie Cole include "God On Trial - Opening Arguments" (openingarguments.org) a radio drama series that exposes the war between God and Satan for the souls of men that explores the question of God's right to rule the world.

Go to www.liferecovery.com for a complete listing.

- facebook.com/LifeRecoveryInc
- twitter.com/LifeRecoveryInc
- youtube.com/LifeRecoveryInc
- instagram.com/LifeRecoveryInc
- pinterest.com/LifeRecoveryInc
- amazon.com/author/LifeRecoveryInc

A Case For Justice: Recovering Lost Blessings

A Case for Justice uncovers the "mysteries of iniquity" that have been buried deep within our bloodlines by tracing the patterns of loss and identifying the places of demonic assault. It unveils the agreements that have been made with the Enemy and disarms the arguments the Accuser of the Brethren has used to build his case against us. It is Guilt and not God who has made his indictment against us and has used his patterns of demonic judgment to swallow up our blessings and to destroy our godly inheritance. The remedy for our sin is not in living a sinless life, but in the shed Blood of the Lamb of God. The Blood of Jesus Christ not only takes away our sin and its effects, but gives us a way to recover lost blessings through forgiveness, repentance and confession. A Case for Justice clarifies how God's system of Divine Justice operates in the Court of Heaven which makes it possible for us to live in the freedom Jesus died to give us.

CRAVINGS -Why Do I Do What I Don't Want To Do?

Craving is defined as a strong desire to have something, to demand, to force, through deviousness. We are torn between self-indulgence and self-control, often spending our lives trying to quit something we cannot seem to stop.

Freedom from the failure and dysfunction brought on by addictions begins with knowing the truth about "who I am". Cravings takes us beyond the surface of addictions and typical "do-more management strategies" and "try harder" self-help methods, into the deeper context of spiritual warfare. It exposes the lies we believe and the operation of demonic programming that controls our souls. The book offers a biblical, in depth look at the spiritual battle that goes on inside of us that makes deliverance a real part of our healing and recovery.

Taking The Devil to Court - Present Your Case (Revised)

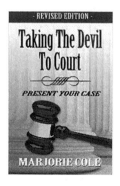

"Taking the Devil to Court" is a basic primer in understanding spiritual warfare. It sets the stage for giving the reader a deeper understanding of the "real life" drama of spiritual warfare and lays a biblical foundation that will adequately explain the most difficult of spiritual entanglements and encounters. "Taking the Devil to Court" is a basic, "must read" for anyone wanting freedom for themselves or for those working to "set captives free".

Several new chapters have been added to address the issues of DNA, programming, and dealing with demonic "alters". "Taking the Devil to Court" also clearly addresses the subtle "first person impersonations of the "strongman" Jesus warned about in Matthew 12:29 and Luke 11, so often overlooked in traditional Christian counseling. Without understanding how the Enemy masquerades as our very thoughts, we will not be able to take every thought captive and make it subject to Christ. (II Cor. 10:3-5).

* * *

Check out www.liferecovery.com for more books, cd's, podcasts, blogs, and videos.

Made in the USA
Middletown, DE
25 November 2022